ODDLY UNJUST

How the OJ Simpson Case Proves God

LARRY HARTMANN

Copyright © 2016 by Larry Hartmann

Oddly Unjust
How the OJ Simpson Case Proves God
by Larry Hartmann

Printed in the United States of America.

ISBN 9781498468220

All rights reserved solely by the author. The author guarantees all contents are original and do not infringe upon the legal rights of any other person or work. No part of this book may be reproduced in any form without the permission of the author. The views expressed in this book are not necessarily those of the publisher.

Unless otherwise indicated, Scripture quotations taken from the New King James Version (NKJV). Copyright © 1982 by Thomas Nelson, Inc. Used by permission. All rights reserved.

www.xulonpress.com

Dedication

This book is dedicated to my wife Laura and my three sons: James, Tyler, and Drew. May this help you better understand my love for all of you and my sometimes-overbearing passion for God.

The book is also dedicated to the hard working team at Impact Paterson, helping the community of Paterson, New Jersey with creating jobs. May this serve as a reminder of our calling to bring the light to every town and to be the good Samaritan to the less fortunate through our jobs ministry. Any net proceeds from this book will go towards funding the not-for-profit ministry supporting job creation in Paterson, NJ. The web site is: www.impactpaterson.com

Table of Contents

Acknowledgments ix
Executive Summary: The OJ Simpson Case, God, Jesus, and
        the Bible 10

Chapter 1: Oddly Unjust – A Fallen Superstar 13
Chapter 2: Trial of the Century 23
Chapter 3: God on Trial 41
Chapter 4: Is There Probable Cause? 51
Chapter 5: Motive and Timeline 65
Chapter 6: The Bible: Admit to Evidence or Unreliable? 83
Chapter 7: The Empty Tomb: Conspiracy or Miracle? 97
Chapter 8: Closing Arguments, Deliberations, and Verdict 109

Conclusion: Are You Still Deliberating? 121
Appendix: Great Sources for More Inspiration 129
About the Author 133

Acknowledgments

Thanks Dr. Larry Keefauver, for your phenomenal editing of this book. You were able to take my passion on this topic and insure we delivered something interesting, engaging, and true to the word.

O.J. Simpson Found Not Guilty[1]

The 1995 murder case of football legend **O.J. Simpson** *was one of the most-explosive media moments in the dawn of the Internet age. From the time news of the killings of Simpson's wife,* **Nicole Brown Simpson***, and friend* **Ronald Goldman** *made the headlines, the case held the attention of the nation in a vice grip. The trial officially began January 24, 1995, in Los Angeles at the California Supreme Court, later moving to the Criminal Courts Building in Santa Monica. Televised almost exclusively by Court TV and several major outlets, the case that prosecutor Simpson amassed a so-called "Dream Team" of attorneys, including* **F. Lee Bailey***,* **Robert Shapiro***, the aforementioned Kardashian, and the late* **Johnny Cochran***.* **On the morning of October 3 at 10:00 a.m., the jury turned in a not-guilty verdict, stopping the entire nation in its tracks as the news broke.**

Executive Summary

The OJ Simpson Case, God, Jesus, and the Bible

This book explores the proof that God exists, the Bible is the truth, and Jesus was indeed God's Son through the lens of the OJ Simpson murder trial. It was seemingly an open and shut murder case with reams of evidence. Yet a Dream Team of lawyers took an impossible case

---

[1] NewsOne Original **news**one.com/2733566/**o-j-simpson**-acquitted

against OJ, with solid evidence and one in seven billion odds that said he did it, and somehow shockingly came away with a not guilty verdict.

The book draws the parallel between the compelling body of evidence we have proving the claims of God, Jesus Christ, and supporting the truths of the Bible and how a "Dream Team" of worldly dis-creditors can blind the eyes to the truth. Referencing many great books that have been written around proving God and Christianity, this book seeks to break that message down so the everyday person and especially today's youth can consider what they believe and why. Using big data and statistics, we will discover what the odds say and what the most logical and reasonable alternatives are to these big issues based on what we know and can prove.

Using the backdrop of and learning from the OJ Simpson murder trial, we will see how even though the motive, timeline, and the physical and scientific evidence all pointed to guilt, he was found not guilty. The persuasion and influence of the Dream Team of lawyers, clouded and distorted the evidence, making seemingly irrefutable guilt turn into a not guilty verdict.

This book will help you determine if Jesus' sentence 2000 years ago was fair and reasonable or **oddly unjust**. If our appeal to the highest court in the land is upheld and the death sentence of Jesus Christ was the biggest miscarriage of justice of all time, then clearly the implications are profound and life changing.

So, let's dig in and examine what the facts tell us, what the proof says, and what the odds show when we apply our modern techniques of evidence, DNA, big data, statistics, and old fashioned logic and reasoning to the conviction of Jesus Christ 2000 years ago.

Was O.J. Simpson guilty or innocent? *Nicole Brown Simpson, and Goldman were found murdered inside her Los Angeles condo on June 13, 1994. Split from her husband two years prior, the former NFL great immediately became a prime suspect. After agreeing to turn himself in to police on June 17th, Simpson never appeared and left behind what experts later determined to be a suicide letter. The letter, read by defense attorney* **Robert Kardashian,** *added a new wrinkle to the case as a city-wide search for Simpson was underway. The trial officially began January 24, 1995, in Los Angeles at the California Supreme Court, later moving to the Criminal Courts Building in Santa Monica. Televised almost exclusively by Court TV and several major outlets, the case that prosecutor* **Marcia Clark** *and District Attorney* **Christopher Darden** *were building looked to be a lock for their side.*[2]

---

[2] http://www.inquisitr.com/2469122/twenty-years-since-o-j-simpson-not-guilty-verdict-those-closest-to-the-case-reflect/

Chapter 1

Oddly Unjust—A Fallen Star

Exactly what happened sometime after ten o'clock on the Sunday night of June 12, 1994 is still disputed, but there was no doubt a tragic murder occurred. Most likely a single male came through the back entrance of Nicole Brown Simpson's condominium in the prestigious Brentwood area of Los Angeles. In a small, nearly enclosed area near the front gate, the man brutally slashed Nicole and then struggled with and repeatedly stabbed Ronald Goldman. Ronald Goldman was a twenty-five-year-old acquaintance of Nicole's who had come to her condominium to return a pair of sunglasses that her mother had left at a local restaurant. It could not have been a random crime, as the anger and passion was easy to see at the brutal crime scene. This was no random murder.

All the evidence gathered would seem to point to an open and shut case that one of the most famous professional football players of the era and well known celebrity, OJ Simpson, had committed the tragic and violent acts. The case against OJ was built, the evidence gathered, and a highly publicized trial began.

Strangely, after a jury of twelve common people spent months listening to the evidence, a suspected killer with a mountain of evidence against him was released with a not guilty verdict. The case has been described as the most publicized criminal trial in American history and many argue, one of the biggest miscarriages of justice of our time.

Beyond a Reasonable Doubt

The standard of finding guilt for OJ was beyond a reasonable doubt. It's estimated that over the past twenty years, authorities have made more than a quarter of a billion arrests with this standard. Once arrested, experts say that 90 percent of criminals plead guilty without ever facing a jury, because they know the evidence is compelling against them. They would be convicted if tried.

So, what is the legal theory of reasonable doubt that makes 90 percent of criminals plead guilty? Here is the definition in simple terms: that no other logical explanation could be found from the facts, except that the defendant committed the crime.

For a jury, this often means considering weeks and months of testimony. Considering motive, timelines, physical evidence, expert witnesses, and hearing directly from the accused, all leading to a final judgement and jury vote. No one single piece of evidence can usually convict; it takes a case. This system works better than any other for deciding innocence and guilt. Our society relies on it for order. It works well a high percentage of the time, even getting criminals to plead guilty before trial. Except, once in a while, it doesn't work.

Was the OJ trial one of those situations?
Did we see firsthand a miscarriage of justice?

Was it sleight of hand by a defense team that fought hard for OJ? Did the jury simply not consider the facts and decide with their hearts? What happened that OJ Simpson could be found innocent?

Now, imagine the system breaking down on national TV during the Trial of the Century. Many asked, how can reasonable people come to unreasonable conclusions? If the expert witnesses proved the DNA odds were one in seven billion of being wrong, odds that would shatter any logical argument of a mistake, how then could a jury doubt the findings and set OJ free? On October 3, 1995, they did.

> **Simpson Free:** *Flanked by Cochran and longtime friend and attorney Robert Kardashian, Simpson stood and faced the jury as a court clerk read two "not guilty" verdicts on October 3, 1995. Members of Simpson's family cried tears of joy in the courtroom as the family of murder victim Ron Goldman wept just a few feet away. The moment was the third most "universally impactful" televised moment of the last 50 years — behind the September 11, 2001, attacks and Hurricane Katrina in 2005 — according to a survey by Nielsen and Sony. Testimony in the trial took about nine months, encompassing about 120 witnesses, 45,000 pages of evidence and 1,100 exhibits.*[3]

---

[3] http://www.inquisitr.com/2469122/twenty-years-since-o-j-simpson-not-guilty-verdict-those-closest-to-the-case-reflect/

What Does the OJ Simpson Case have to do with Christianity?

What could we possible draw from this perceived gross miscarriage of justice that would enlighten us further on God, Jesus Christ, faith, and the Bible?

In 1995, a jury set free a famous, legendary athlete who was guilty. Some 2000 years ago, a Roman court of law along with a religious mob convicted a man to death. He was no ordinary man, he was Jesus Christ. What was His crime? He healed the sick, He raised the dead, He fed the hungry, and He comforted the weary. Jesus did amazing things, but He also claimed to be God's Son.

Masses followed Him and His words changed a society until the old line religious leaders of the day decided He was too disruptive and quite dangerous to the status quo. He claimed to be God, He healed people on the holy Sabbath, and He updated the message of the Torah to one of God's amazing love through His Son. For this, He was tried, beaten, and crucified. He never recanted His claims. His crime was claiming to be God. Blasphemy in the highest order, argued the religious leaders of the day. Jesus never flinched, He went to His death for these claims.

The parallels to examining the existence of God and Christianity through the trial that took place 2000 years ago and the OJ trial can be an enlightening lens to consider closely what the evidence really says in both trials.

Both cases represent a great and public miscarriage of justice. However, Jesus' conviction and trial for claiming to be the Son of God has not yet exceeded the statute of limitations for an appeal—an appeal that can now examine new data, testimony, and proof. We can now deploy big data and analytics to assess the odds of His claims and better question expert witnesses.

Many people wonder how reasonable people can come to unreasonable conclusions. How could the OJ Simpson trial result in an innocent verdict with so much overwhelming evidence and a clear motive? We will look at that case and determine how such a thing could have happened.

Christ's appeal has broader implications for all of us. Either Jesus was the Son of God or He was a fraud and deserved to be punished for His outlandish claims. With a topic so important and with eternal consequences, this appeal must be taken to the highest court in the land and a new verdict reached.

The Appeal of the Guilty Verdict of Jesus Christ

In the United States legal system, defendants have various rights to appeal a court decision. If someone is convicted of murder, for example, before that person can be put to death, there are exhaustive levels of appeals that will be heard. Our system tries to insure all possible arguments are listened to and considered in an effort to protect the innocent who might have been convicted. There are designed to try to right a wrong that might have occurred in a lower court.

The highest court and final word if all else fails is the Supreme Court. They receive about 10,000 requests each year to consider important cases, but only agree to hear about eighty.

If a person is deemed not guilty in a criminal trial, they cannot be tried again. For OJ, his verdict was not open to review. For Jesus Christ, His guilty verdict is still open for review so we will take it to the highest court in the land to appeal.

We will ask the same question in this appeal that Pontius Pilate and the Jewish leaders considered. Was Jesus God's Son? 2000 years ago, the courts ruled He was not, in a hasty and ill-conceived legal process.

However, if He was God's Son, His words and His message change everything. We will need to dig deeper into many important issues in this appeal.

Is there even a God? If we can't prove there is a God, then by default, there is no God's Son, so case closed.

Is the Bible reliable evidence? If we prove there is a God based on the words of the Bible, then we need to examine the Bible itself and see if the courts would deem this as reliable.

Was Jesus truly the Messiah? We will then proceed to examine if Jesus was truly the Messiah, the Savior, the one foretold in the Torah and Old Testament as God's only Son.

All three have to be proven in order to have a chance to win the appeal. If we can't prove God exists, case closed. If the Bible is just a collection of old stories and tales and nothing more, we are arguing on shaky ground and our appeal will be dismissed. If Jesus did not fulfill all of the prophecies of the Old Testament and change the lives of the world, if we find any flaws in the Jesus story, the appeal will be rejected.

- *Is there even a God?*
- *Is the Bible reliable evidence?*
- *Was Jesus truly the Messiah?*

You as a Supreme Court Justice

A Supreme Court justice team is ideally made up of people with many different world views, political leanings, and experiences. As you consider this journey to review with fresh eyes the evidence, you might be a Supreme Court justice who just does not believe in God at all and cannot support religion and a god you can't prove.

You might be a justice who was raised in a Christian family, but as you grew older and formed your own opinions you found reasons to doubt your faith. Did God really flood the earth and Noah actually put all those animals in an ark? If God is a loving God, why is there so much suffering? What about that young child in the wilds of Africa who never hears about Jesus? What happens to that person?

Maybe you come from the view that all roads do lead to God and you can worship and find Him in your own way. When this life ends, if you're a good person and you try to do the right things, a loving God will surely have mercy on you. Or maybe you have followed other religious traditions and have been turned off by all of this God stuff and are confused. Maybe the issue of the Christian world view of homosexuality has turned you away entirely from the loving words of Jesus. Maybe you have been turned off by the Christians themselves, who seem to always disappoint and not live up to the words they seem to preach. No matter what type of justice you might be, this case welcomes your view as you decide the outcome of this appeal.

Proving Jesus and Christianity beyond a Reasonable Doubt

While it's been said that it is not possible for human beings to absolutely prove anything, it *might just be* possible to build a compelling and logical case for God's existence. Then we *might just* be able to follow the evidence to prove Jesus Christ might actually be God's Son and voice to the world. We need proof that could hold up to the legal standard, proving it beyond a reasonable doubt based on the preponderance of the evidence, the facts when viewed in total, and considering the timelines, prophecies, and physical evidence in our universe. Having a strong cross examination on the claims of Christianity might change the verdict.

> **While blind faith and feelings about God work for some, asking the tough questions, considering the evidence, and forming your own educated decision is something everyone should do when it comes to God.**

So, just like the jury in the OJ Simpson trial, this verdict on the appeal of Christ will fall on your vote. The verdict on God, the Bible, and Jesus Christ will be determined by you and you alone. You can disagree with your fellow justices and have your own vote. Even if the other Supreme Court justices decide differently, your decision and your vote counts. However, before you cast your vote, you should probably grapple first with the following questions.

Why would God have done all this?
Do the timelines fit or do we find gaps that discredit the story?
What about the physical and scientific evidence?
Can we believe the expert witnesses and consider their credibility and views?
What did they see and witness?
Is this credible testimony and believable or should it be discounted as hearsay?
Can statistics and big data help us handicap the matter?
What do the odd's makers say about these events?
If we use the Bible as evidence, does it stand up to the tests or is it just a collections of old stories written by men?
Can the defense team on this appeal raise enough arguments to reverse the decision the Roman Courts made 2000 years ago?

Take some time to hear all of the evidence and decide how you would vote if you were on the biggest Supreme Court case in history.

Consider what the evidence says and if this appeal should right what many call the greatest wrong in world history.

> "The difference between faith and superstition is that the first uses reason to go as far as it can and then makes the jump; the second shuns reason entirely—which is why superstition is not the ally, but the enemy of true religion."
> – Syndy Harris

Dig in and Examine What the Facts Tell Us

Take some time to hear all of the evidence before you decide how you would vote if you were on the biggest Supreme Court case in history. Don't shun reason and don't fear looking at both sides of an argument. Seek the best and most logical answer. Get ready to consider the case with an open yet questioning mind. Consider what the evidence says and if this appeal should right what many call the greatest wrong in world history.

Do you remember watching the OJ Simpson trial?
What were your initial thoughts when you heard the not guilty verdict?
Have you read the account of the trial of Jesus Christ? (Matthew 26:36-27:31)
What at your initial thoughts on His trial and guilty verdict?

Book cover for *If I Did It*, with "If" in very small print, embedded in the word "I"

"On March 13, 2007, a judge prevented Simpson from receiving any further compensation from the defunct book deal and TV interview. He ordered the bundled book rights to be auctioned. In August 2007, a Florida bankruptcy court awarded the rights to the book to the Goldman family to partially satisfy an unpaid civil judgment. Originally titled *If I Did It*, the book was renamed *If I Did It: Confessions of the Killer*, with the word 'If' reduced in size to make it appear that the title was, *I Did It: Confessions of the Killer*. Additional material was added by members of the Goldman family, investigative journalist Dominick Dunne, and author Pablo Fenjves. The Goldman family was listed as the author."[4]

---

[4] The Goldman Family (2007). *If I Did It: Confessions of the Killer*. Beaufort Books. ISBN 978-0-8253-0588-7. Archived from the original on May 11, 2008. Retrieved July 1, 2010.

Chapter 2

Trial of the Century

OJ Simpson was an icon. He was a star athlete, actor, and sports announcer. He was bigger than big. Born Orenthal James Simpson, he was known as OJ. Like many star athletes, he had an interesting journey to stardom and success. At the age of two, OJ Simpson contracted rickets, leaving him pigeon-toed and his legs skinny and bow-legged. He had to wear a pair of shoes connected by an iron bar for a few hours almost every day until he was five years old. Almost like the fictional Forrest Gump.

OJ's parents separated when he was a young boy. Along with a brother and two sisters, he was raised by his mother in California. He lived in the rugged, largely black Potrero Hill district of San Francisco. O.J. traveled a rough road in his journey out of the projects of Petrero Hill to stardom.

When he was thirteen, he joined a gang called the Persian Warriors. He could have gone either way in his life. A fight led to his first brush with the legal system, as he had to spend a week at the San Francisco Youth Guidance Center in 1962. Luckily for OJ, he later found meaning and direction through football and left the life of gangs and trouble behind, for a while. There were few opportunities for the poor in this area. It was said that black kids were welcome at the local gym near him and that's where he most spent time. This opened a door to his legendary success in football.

OJ played football at Galileo High School where he was a star. While he was still not recruited to a major college after his high school exploits, he attended a junior college in San Francisco, where he broke many running back records. After this success, he was then on the radar screens of the major colleges and he was heavily recruited. USC won the derby and OJ became their star running back. As a USC Trojan, he gained fame as a two-time All-American halfback for USC, setting NCAA records and winning the famed Heisman Trophy as College Football's Best player. He led USC to winning the Rose Bowl. OJ now had it all and his future looked even brighter.

When the NFL draft was conducted, OJ was the first overall pick in the entire draft by the Buffalo Bills in 1969. Life could not get any better. Being the number one pick meant instant financial security. He went on to continue his amazing success, earning the nickname, "The Juice." OJ topped 1,000 yards rushing over five consecutive years (1972–76) and led the National Football League in rushing yards four times. In 1973, he became the first player in NFL history to rush for more than 2,000 yards in a single season, adding another amazing accomplishment to his football legacy.

After completing his highly esteemed football career with the San Francisco Forty-niners and retiring from professional football in 1979, OJ found a second act. Simpson moved on to a profitable career as a sportscaster and an actor. Ironically, he played a man framed for murder by the police in the film *The Klansman*. Simpson also appeared in the *Naked Gun* film comedies, playing a dim-witted assistant detective, and regularly appeared in TV commercials for the Hertz rental-car company, where he was seen leaping over luggage and other obstacles in an effort to catch a flight. Additionally, he worked as a commentator for *Monday Night Football*. OJ was known and respected by all. He was a true American hero and success story. He could pitch any product and had a million dollar smile and personal brand.

Unfortunately, he will remembered for something quite different. Something evil, violent, and unthinkable. On June 12, 1994, everything changed for OJ Simpson and for his legion of adoring fans and admirers.

The Other OJ

On June 12, Nicole Brown Simpson, OJ Simpson's former wife and her friend, Ronald Goldman, were found knifed to death outside her condo in the wealthy Los Angeles neighborhood of Brentwood. It was a bloody and violent crime scene.

The Police investigation quickly focused on Simpson. Evidence emerged that he had beaten and threatened his former wife in the past. Pictures emerged of his ex-wife showing domestic violence at the hands of OJ. The public smiling persona of OJ quickly changed to a more sobering and darker view of an abuser with a dark side.

As the police investigation kicked into high gear, the evidence was right in front of them. The team quickly found blood spots on his driveway and a bloody glove and sock on his property. OJ also had a clear cut on his hand. He could not account for his whereabouts at the time of the crime. There was a lapse in his alibi. The evidence quickly piled up against him and all indicators pointed to an angry ex-spouse who murdered his wife and took out Ron Goldman as collateral damage, as his rage exploded. The violent nature of the killings pointed to a crime of passion.

Several factors heightened and complicated the drama as OJ had a mixed-race marriage in a nation that had lingering stigma from interracial marriage. He was the murder suspect of a Los Angeles Police Department that had a reputation for racism and corruption that had boiled over.

Simpson also was a wealthy Hollywood actor and ad pitchman with little connection to the black community, a man who divorced his black wife for a young blonde and traveled in Los Angeles' most privileged white circles. His money and fame placed him far from the poor, black men languishing in the criminal justice system.

An investigation was hastily conducted and in the span of one week the case was seemingly made. The evidence all pointed to OJ Simpson as the killer. The papers carried the details of the drama every day and the TV stations featured every new bit of information as the leading story. The nation was obsessed with the OJ story. Murder charges were filed against him and OJ's legal team agreed to have him give himself up at 12:00 PM, ironically High Noon, on Friday of the following week.

However, by 2:00 p.m., OJ was missing. He failed to show up to turn himself in and a massive manhunt was underway. His lawyer, Robert Kardashian, read reporters an apparent suicide note from Simpson. Then, from 6 p.m. to 8 p.m. on that Friday evening, the nation watched the famous white bronco car chase with OJ and his friend as they drove through Los Angeles Freeways, from Orange County while a line of police cars with lights flashing followed behind. The spectacle escalated as the public began lining up on freeway overpasses to cheer and wave as the surreal and dark OJ Simpson parade made its way through various parts of Los Angeles. It was a spectacle like no other with the outcome unknown. Many speculated OJ would kill himself and the story would end with the car chase. It finally ended when OJ surrendered as he pulled into his home in Los Angeles. He was arrested for the murders of Nicole Brown Simpson and Ron Goldman.

The Infamous OJ Simpson Trial

A trial would follow with results that would shock a nation. A jury of twelve peers were selected to hear the case. It seemed like an open and shut case with no hope for OJ Simpson.

A grand jury was assembled to decide if they case should go forward, but in a strange twist, the judge ruled that the publicity and media frenzy from the trial made this grand jury process tainted and decided to conduct a "probable cause" hearing, with a judge deciding instead of a jury on the matters at hand.

After the hearing found probable cause, a jury of eight women and four men was selected. The panel included eight blacks, one white, one Hispanic, and two people of mixed race.

Motive

Establishing a motive for a crime is a cornerstone of any criminal case. Why would OJ Simpson do this?

The answer was not good for the defense. It was established OJ was angry at his ex-wife for breaking up with him a second time. They had divorced; then she had sought a reconciliation more than a year earlier. He had agreed, but she changed her mind again a month before the murders by returning his birthday gift. On the day of the murder, he was excluded from the family circle at the dance recital for his kids and the dinner afterwards. Simpson was angry and withdrawn, as witnesses would later testify.

He also had a patterned history of domestic violence, proven through calls to 911 and pictures kept by Nicole Brown Simpson. It was clear OJ had an angry side, was angry at his ex-wife, and had a history of violence. Motive was established. The defense could not argue. Strike One for the Prosecutor.

Timeline

Based on trial testimony and other reports, the murder took place between 10:00 p.m. and 10:45 p.m. on the day in question. What would the proof show? Here is a recap of the evening:

- 4:45–O.J. arrives for his kids recital, sitting behind Nicole and the Brown family.
- 6:15–After the recital, O.J. talks, laughs with the Brown family
- 6:30-7:00–Nicole and party arrive at the restaurant Mezzaluna. At OJ's Rockingham estate, O.J. tells his friend Kaelin he's angry about Nicole wearing a tight dress and not allowing him to go to the restaurant.
- 8:30–Nicole leaves restaurant.
- 9:00 – A friend of Nicole, Faye Resnick calls her from a drug rehabilitation center. She reports Nicole told Simpson: "Get away from us! Get out of my life. You're not welcome with this family anymore."
- 9:03 – Kato Kaelin, OJ's roommate, calls his friend Tom O'Brien, but is interrupted by O.J., who needs $20 for dinner.
- 9:10–O.J. and Kaelin go to McDonald's to get food, driving O.J.'s Bentley.

- 9:25–Kaelin pays for the meals. O.J. eats as they drive home.
- 9:33 – Ron Goldman ends his work shift at the restaurant
- 9:35–Kaelin leaves O.J. standing near the Bentley at estate.
- 9:45–Nicole calls Mezzaluna to check on her sunglasses that she'd left behind. She talks to Karen Lee Crawford and Ron Goldman. He takes the glasses, goes home and changes before driving six blocks to Nicole's condominium.
- 9:45 or 9:50–Rosa Lopez, domestic worker in the house next to Simpson's, hears O.J.'s dog barking.
- 10:15–Nicole's neighbors hear dog barking. Prosecutors say this is the time of the killings.
- 10:22–Limousine driver Allan Park arrives at Rockingham to take O.J. to airport for a trip to Chicago. He waits at the car on a side street.
- 10:40–Park pulls up to Rockingham, rings the buzzer three or four times, gets no answer. Also, resident near Nicole's home reports hearing someone shout, "Hey" three times.
- 10:40-10:45–Kaelin, hears thumps on his wall near air conditioner at the home.
- 10:43 – The limo Driver, Park tries to page his boss, Dale St. John to say no one is answering at the estate.
- 10:55–Park sees Kaelin near the house, and a tall African-American figure walks up to the front door.
- 10:56–Kaelin admits Park to estate.
- 11:01-11:02–O.J. comes out of the house to board the limo. He joins Kaelin in brief search for a possible intruder related to thumping noise.
- 11:10-11:15–Park and O.J. leave for the airport.

- 11:40–Sukru Boztepe, a neighbor of Schwab, takes Nicole's dog, and notices red spots on the dog's paws and legs.
- 11:45–O.J. leaves for Chicago on American Airlines Flight 668.
- Midnight–Boztepe and his wife, Bettina Rasmussen, take the dog for a walk. He leads them to Nicole's condo. They find the bodies at 12:10.

OJ could not account for the 90 minutes between 9:30 when he left Kaelin and 11:01 the time of the murders. The timeline and events of the day fit like a glove. The evidence continued to mount. The facts pointed even more towards OJ Simpson. Strike two.

What about Physical Evidence?

A solid motive and an airtight timeline are compelling, but having physical evidence is important. In the OJ trial, there was overwhelming and convincing physical proof.

A left-handed blood-soaked high end men's glove and ski cap were found at the murder scene, and what seemed to be the right-hand blood soaked match to that glove was found in the outside walkway behind Simpson's house.

Fibers on the ski cap matched fibers in the fabric in the Bronco, and similar fibers were found on the gloves and on Ron Goldman's shirt. The glove at Rockingham contained a blond hair that could have come from Nicole and a dark hair that could have come from Ron Goldman. The theory was that Simpson lost the cap and left-handed glove during the murders, and after losing the glove, sustained a cut on his left index finger.

The theory was that once the murders were done, he rushed back to his house in the Bronco, carelessly parking it on Rockingham while the Limo Driver, Allan Park, waited at the Ashford Street entrance to the house. Simpson entered the grounds and tried to sneak down the walkway alongside the house, intending to bury or hide the clothing and knife used in the murders. In the dark, he bumped into the air-conditioning unit, which accounted for the noises Kato Kaelin heard, and dropped the glove at that moment. Minutes later, he entered the house and turned on the lights, buzzed the gate to let Park in, and then left for the airport.

In addition to a suitcase and a bag of golf clubs, Simpson carried a black golf bag that he insisted on taking into the limousine himself. That bag was never seen again.

A bloody shoe print at the crime scheme was determined to come from a size 12 Italian dress shoe made by Bruno Magli. Records showed OJ had purchased such a rare and expensive shoe in that size. Records showed only 300 pairs of this specific brand model and size were sold in the entire United States. The shoes alone would seem to be enough evidence to convict. How many murderers wear Bruno Magli size 12 shoes and own high end men's gloves that could have committed the crime?

The investigators had done their job: *strike three based on the physical evidence.*

Scientific Evidence: One is Seven Billion Odds

Last was the scientific evidence. Surely science could shed further light on the investigation. With so much blood at the crime scene, on the gloves, and in OJ's bronco, it would seem that the DNA testing would clearly be the last straw to put OJ away for life. Here are the highlights of the scientific evidence presented at the trial:

1) DNA tests of traces of blood discovered inside the Bronco matched O.J. Simpson, Nicole Brown Simpson, and Ron Goldman. How could this blood have gotten inside the Bronco, especially Ron Goldman's blood?
2) Blood on the glove found at the Simpson residence tested positively for all three: OJ, Nicole, and Ron Brown.
3) A sock found on the floor of Simpson's bedroom had a spot of blood that produced a DNA match for Nicole Brown Simpson.
4) Blood drops on the sidewalk at the murder scene, on the walkway, and hallway at Rockingham matched O.J. Simpson's blood.

This DNA evidence was presented over a period of many weeks in June, July, and August by expert witnesses. The testimony was that only one in seven billion people would be expected to have the alleles observed in the crime scene sample and in the defendant. One in seven billion odds just on the blood and DNA evidence. Who could doubt the findings? Certainly this was the fourth strike that would close the case quickly.

Plot Twist: Enter the Dream Team

OJ did have one very clear advantage that changed things in this trial. With his wealth and celebrity power, he assembled a legal team that became known as the Dream Team to defend him. The title was not hyperbole; it was justified. This was a unique collection of very powerful men. The lawyers that led the Dream Team included, Johnnie L. Cochran Jr., F. Lee Bailey, Robert Shapiro, Robert Kardashian, and

Alan Dershowitz. The résumés and credentials of the Dream Team were amazing.

It was F. Lee Bailey who won convicted murderer Sam Sheppard a retrial and an eventual not guilty verdict. The story of Sheppard, who was accused of killing his wife, eventually was adapted as "The Fugitive," a successful '60s TV show as well as a 1993, Harrison Ford-starring film.

Alan Dershowitz was one of the most famous lawyers in the United States. He was no stranger to nationally known cases, whether it was the pornography-fueled "Deep Throat" case that touched on First Amendment issues or the Claus Von Bulow case, which was later explored in the Jeremy Irons-starring movie "Reversal Of Fortune." Alan was a legal rock star.

Johnnie Cochran was a very well-known lawyer before the Simpson case, renowned for his skills as well as his infectious personality. After the OJ Simpson trial, which he was the most visible of this amazing Dream Team, he became a national celebrity, frequently appearing on news shows. He became the "go-to" lawyer for the rich and famous, representing celebrities such as Sean Combs, Michael Jackson, and more.

Robert Shapiro was a solid lawyer, but not as wellknown as the others. He went on to become one of the early founders and shareholders of Legal Zoom, an online legal service business that boomed based on his celebrity status. In 2013, the National Law Journal named him to the list of The 100 Most Influential Lawyers in America.

Robert Kardashian was OJ's family lawyer and friend. He was also the first Kardashian to appear on television years before the reality TV family become known to the world through "Keeping up with the Kardashians."

It was a Dream Team, the best legal team ever assembled, representing a criminal case against all odds. They were facing off against the prosecutors, two humble lawyers, Chris Darden and Marcia Clark, who work for the State with much less financial resources. These prosecutors were there to present the case to the jury and win what seemed like a simple open and shut case. Suddenly, they were presented with a David versus Goliath setting. The world waited in anticipation.

The Dream Team's Strategy

This was the trial of the century and the All Star Dream Team rose to the occasion, relishing in crafting a creative defense against all odds. This was the super bowl of trials and the Dream Team came to counter-attack on all fronts and win.

First, it argued that the Prosecution was wrong about O.J. Simpson's motive, mood, appearance, and behavior. Simpson did not want to harm Nicole, and was in fact not angry at her. They provided their arguments around happy family videos of OJ, softening the Prosecution's portrayal.

Second, and more importantly, they argued that the racists LA cops had conspired to frame OJ Simpson and planted the evidence at the scene. They trapped witnesses into making personal statements, which they later disproved, creating credibility questions. They attacked the personal character of the policemen who did the work and created enough doubt to make the jury question them.

The Dream Team won a big battle when the Prosecution team decided to have OJ Simpson try on the actual gloves from the murder scene, which matched his size. The problem was, OJ was wearing a thin protective plastic glove liner to protect the evidence and when he tried to slip his hand into the glove, it did not fit. The famous line, "If the gloves don't fit, you have to acquit," cited by Johnny Cochran, would ring in the ears of the jury throughout their deliberations. A big tactical error by the Prosecution allowed this mistake to happen.

Third, the Dream Team attacked the DNA evidence. The experts showed 1-7 Billion odds of a match to OJ. How could this be refuted? The Dream Team demonstrated to the court that mistakes were made in collecting the blood and that the samples could have been mixed up or "cross contaminated" at the crime scene or in the laboratory. Paid experts testified that there was just "something wrong" with much of the DNA evidence, especially the trace of blood in the sock that matched Nicole Brown Simpson. Again, they created a small bit of doubt despite the overwhelming evidence with the DNA. The Dream Team was hitting on all cylinders, against all odds and creating doubt.

Closing Arguments

Persuasive communicators can convince people of most anything. They can make facts seem like fiction, fiction seem like fact, and easily create doubt.

The Dream Team argued the unthinkable and then communicated in a way that was totally believable. These were gifted men. Here are some excerpts from the closing arguments by the Dream Team:

"This is O. J. Simpson's one day in court. By your decision you control his very life in your hands. Treat it carefully. Treat it fairly. Be fair. Don't be part of this continuing cover-up. Do the right thing. Remember, if it doesn't fit, you must acquit. If these messengers have lied to you, you can't trust their message. This has been a search for truth and no matter how bad it looks, if truth is out there on a scaffold, and wrong is in here on the throne, remember that the scaffold always sways the future and beyond the dim unknown standeth the same God for all people keeping watch above his own. He watches all of us. And he'll watch you in your decision. Thank you for your attention. God bless you."

The Deliberation and Shocking Verdict

With all the facts and interesting theories, experts pontificated the jury could certainly spend a few days if not weeks considering this case. Shockingly, the jury of twelve deliberated for only four hours. After a trial that was televised for more than 135 days with so many issues to consider, how could the jury have reached a verdict so quickly? The Charles Manson murder trials, with similar assumptions of guilt, took nine days. The famous Melendez brothers' case was debated for twenty-five days before a mistrial and the second trial took twenty days.

Experts weighed in but still wondered. This entire case was strange from the start. So, with the biggest TV audience, estimated to be 150 million people watching, the results would soon be known. It surely must be a guilty verdict despite the valiant effort by the Dream Team to mount an admirable defense.

With anticipation like no other, the verdict was revealed, OJ Simpson was found, "Not Guilty." Despite having a clear motive, putting aside the airtight timeline, even weighing the damning physical evidence and the convincing scientific proof, the jury felt they could not convict beyond a reasonable doubt. With experts telling them the odds on just the DNA alone were one in 7 Billion, OJ Simpson was found not guilty.

That same day, Simpson was acquitted of the criminal charges and set free. The world seemed to let out a collective gasp. How could this have happened, how oddly unjust.

The jury had 135 days of focused court time to only think of this case, yet they whiffed on the final verdict.

Post Log: Strange Justice

OJ was subsequently found liable in a civil wrongful death action brought by the survivors of the two victims. OJ ironically went on to write a book entitled, *If I Did It*, where he told how he hypothetically would have committed the murders. Some felt it was his confession.

While he was free for many years, on the night of September 13, 2007, a group of men led by Simpson broke into a hotel room and stole various sports memorabilia at gunpoint. Three days later, on September 16, 2007, Simpson was arrested for his involvement in the robbery and held without bail. He admitted taking the items, which he said had been stolen from him, but denied breaking into the room. October 3, 2008, exactly thirteen years to the day after he was acquitted of the murders of his wife, Nicole Brown, and Ronald Goldman, OJ was found guilty of all ten new charges and was sentenced to thirty-three years in prison with eligibility for parole in nine years. He is incarcerated at the Lovelock Correctional Center in Lovelock, Nevada through 2017.

Dig in and Examine What the Facts Tell Us

A key to any review is to consider all of the evidence, not just one piece to get the full picture. Then, after you consider it all, cast your vote. Context is important. Just like the OJ trial, one area would not be enough.

If we started with just motive with OJ, we would assume he was likely guilty, but could not convict on that alone. If we just looked at the timeline, it would seem like it points to OJ, but that's not enough to convict. The physical evidence, without the context of the motive and timeline, would be compelling but still not convincing. Simply arguing the DNA and odds of the case might be enough for some, but not all.

However, when you consider the whole picture, the full set of issues in the OJ trial, the story starts to fit together and your vote if you were the juror would have been easy. So what happened?

Was the OJ trial one of those situations where we simply had a miscarriage of justice?
Did the jury simply not consider the facts and decide with their hearts?
Were they lazy in their deliberations?
Did the truth, staring them in the face, conflict with their hearts and minds?
Was the Dream Team the reason things went OJ's way?
Can smart men argue issues that make no sense and win the minds of the listeners?

THE CASE FOR CHRIST.

The former Chicago Tribune legal editor, with a journalist's tenacity, questioned Christian scholars and experts with tough, point-blank questions:

How reliable is the New Testament?
Does evidence for Jesus exist outside the Bible?
Is there any reason to believe the resurrection was an actual historical event?
He shares how his search brought him to this conclusion:
Jesus of Nazareth really is the Son of God.[5]

---

[5] http://www.leestrobel.com/store.php

Chapter 3

God on Trial

While the OJ case was a big one, there is an even bigger issue for all of us to consider and ponder that should get the same attention and more. It is the question of God, faith, belief, and the eternal consequences of our faith and actions.

Why not learn from the OJ trial and apply these principles to your own review as you ponder objectively the evidence and arguments on both sides about God, Jesus, and Christianity.

Any solid faith should be able withstand the tough questions. So, to prove Christianity to an objective jury, the case must first prove God exists. If this can be established, then the question of establishing the Bible is God's Word would make sense. If so, then what does this mean about a Messiah and Jesus Christ?

If this all lines up as arguably logical and sound, then perhaps Christianity could withstand the heat from the Dream Team arguing the other side of this issue.

However, the Dream Team defense is well funded and smart. Some of the brightest and best minds of the history of world join the arguments to say you cannot prove God. The Dream Team has an army of resources and a powerful leader who will go all in to win the case, one person at a time.

The Biggest Trial of All Time

This Dream Team in this appeal is made up of atheists, historians, scientists, and philosophers. They will continue to defend the arguments that there is no God, so by default, Jesus cannot be God's Son; thus, there is no basis for Christianity. You can expect to hear every possible obstacle to the arguments about God. Expect to have witnesses character attacked to take away from their testimony. Don't let that stop you in the search for truth, as the opposition is strong, gifted, and persuasive. It will take clear thinking to sift through the arguments.

According to the Bible, wisdom will be given by God to those who ask. God has promised to reveal himself to those who truly seek him. If you are already a seeker but want to be better convinced, ask God now for wisdom and for him to reveal himself to you. If you are a doubter, try anyway! Ask God to reveal himself to you in a way you have not known him.

Many academically brilliant and gifted people have written and spoken on the proof of God and why Christianity is true. From Josh McDowell in *Evidence Demands a Verdict*, to Lee Stroebel in the *Case for Christ*, and most recently, J Warner Wallace in *Cold Case Christianity*. Amazing and talented authors and speakers have presented proof of faith and God in powerful and well researched messages.

For me, as a businessman, who has read and digested many of these great books, I was persuaded in my own journey to validate my faith. Having grown up in a Christian family, later in life I was challenged with why I believe what I believe and why I thought I was right. Those close to me would argue I was a Christian because my family raised me that way. I heard many arguments like, "Don't all roads lead to God? You Christians are very judgmental thinking you are the only way to God."

I jumped headlong into Christian Apologetics, which are the reasoned arguments or writings in justification of something, typically a theory or religious doctrine. Many of the books were very technical, written by Ivy League trained scientists and top theologians with deep educations. They were not easy reads for the everyday person, but they contained great wisdom.

My personal journey was as a data-driven businessman. My first business was a success that was built on data and modeling of information to make informed credit decisions. The business grew, went public, and later was sold to a Dow 30 company. At the core of this business was data, analytics, and facts to make good decisions on lending money. My current business is a high end retained executive recruiting business, where the application of fact based hiring is our unique differentiator.

Data has always spoken to me, from a kid looking at batting averages and ERAs to statistics and odds in making smart decisions. I remember when I was just ten years old and a fan of basic stats. Alex Johnson was a star hitter for the Angels. During the 1970 season, Johnson hit the ground running in California, leading the league with a .366 batting average through May. He cooled off as the 1970 season progressed, but still went into the All-star break with an average of .328 to earn selection to the A.L. squad. He remained in the batting title race throughout the season, and went into the final game of the season with a batting average which was .002 behind Boston's Carl Yastrzemski, a very small margin for deciding the batting champion. In that final game, Johnson went two-for-three to win the A.L. batting title by a mere 0.0004 over the legendary Carl Yastrzemski. I remember clearly when he was removed from the game after his third at-bat in the seventh inning to insure the title and not risk an out, where his average would have dipped below Yaz's. Stats began to speak to me early that day when I calculated what would have happened if he made an out and lost the batting title to Yaz.

It was natural that I would look to the data and odds about God. The data was there for the taking, but many just would not take the time to consider it. To me, if the God options were laid out in odds and probabilities, everyone would be an instant believer. It's overwhelming. If things were only this simple.

My goal is simply to condense and reduce the arguments that exist from the best writers and speakers on the issues, in the context of a simple appeal of the ruling 2000 years ago to kill Jesus Christ. The greatest wrong was done when Jesus Christ was killed. It was oddly unjust.

To my mind, the facts of the OJ Simpson trial provided overwhelming proof of his guilt. Any one of the pieces of evidence could have hung him out to dry, but the entire body of evidence coupled with his history and motives, made it a slam dunk guilty case. The fact he went free always troubled me.

It was not so much that a murderer was set free, it was how could a jury who heard the evidence and understood the odds, even consider freeing him?

So, as a student of various world religions and beliefs and as someone that was challenged to know what and why they believe regarding faith, I found a metaphor of sorts in the OJ Simpson case and Christ's trial that seemed worth exploring and studying.

What do the odds point to?
Will Christianity make sense, beyond a reasonable doubt?
What were the motives of God?
What does the timelines of the Bible tell us?

Trial Context: Who Was Jesus?

We will start with a bit of context and history. 2000+ years ago, a Jewish boy named Jesus was born. He lived a simple life like many other boys born in those days. However, at the age twenty-eight, something happened to Jesus and he became quite a celebrity in his own right as he went from a simple carpenter to a highly controversial "counter culture celebrity " that changed the world.

His fame happened quickly as the word spread about his amazing teachings, miracles, and healings, in a day with no Twitter, Instagram or Facebook. The story of Jesus spread by word of mouth and it started to create a real buzz. Jesus started his ministry by ironically turning water to wine. He went on to heal the sick, raise the dead, walk on water, and feed 5000 people from a few baskets of fish and bread.

While the miracles astonished the crowds, his most important impact was teaching a new simple faith: Love God with all your heart and love your neighbor. These were the greatest two commandments, taking precedence over the Old Testament Ten Commandments and the over 600 laws and rules of the Torah and Old Testament that governed how the religious were to act and behave at the time.

Love Replaced Rules

Unlike the holy rolling religious leaders of that day, Jesus chose to spend time with the sinners instead of the holy; corrupt tax collectors, prostitutes, and hated Roman soldiers. He chose to help those in need and were unchurched and not following God. He cared about people. He preached that he would leave the ninety-nine sheep in his care to find one lost sheep. The value of every person was clearly taught by him.

The legend of Jesus spread like wildfire. He gained paparazzi and big crowds as even the current religious establishment followed him everywhere to see what was going on and what would be next. The Pharisees and Sadducees, who very legalist Jewish leaders, did not embrace his popularity and claims. They viewed him as a threat to the status quo and did not even consider he could be the Messiah the Torah and Old Testament prophets talked about. They did not see Jesus as the fulfillment of their own holy teachings. As Jesus rebuked their judgmental and pious ways, he focused the crowds on the true message of God. The divide between Jesus and the old religious guard continued growing.

The leaders saw him as a "divisive and dangerous" person, who could disrupt their longstanding beliefs and rules. They did not believe he was God in the form of his son as he claimed, so they conspired to eliminate this radical and have him tried and killed.

As the world knows from the story of the crucifixion, the religious leaders of the time brought him to the courts and argued he should be crucified. When pressed by the Roman leaders as to why, they claimed he was a liar, blasphemer, and dangerous distraction to society. They strongly asserted that Jesus should die, because he claimed to be the Son of God and he certainly wasn't.

The Roman legal system sided with the public pressure and agreed to have Jesus killed for his alleged false claims. The proof to set him free was in front of their very own eyes, but the courts, the legal system, and the accusers did not take the time to reflect on who Jesus was and refused to follow the evidence to make a decision.

He was tried in a kangaroo court and found guilty of blasphemy. The penalty was death on the cross. The single biggest miscarriage of justice in the history of the world had just occurred. Jesus was brutally tortured and crucified like a murderer. The world was never the same after that day when a miscarriage of justice was carried out.

While most crimes have a statute of limitations to argue for a reversal and to file appeals, in this case, that deadline has not yet expired. For the trial of God, the statute of limitations is infinity.

So, our motion on appeal is to throw out the verdict as a miscarriage of justice and a farce. We petition the courts to conduct a new trial, with fresh evidence and new facts as we now know them. We want to have it heard at the highest level, the Supreme Court.

Dig in and Examine What the Facts Tell Us

When pressed by the Roman leaders as to why, the religious leaders claimed this man Jesus was a liar, a blasphemer, and a dangerous distraction to society. They strongly asserted that Jesus should die, because he had been subverting their nation, opposed paying taxes to Caesar, and claimed to be the Christ.

To prepare for this appeal, you need to read the account of the arrest and trial of Jesus Christ in Luke 22:47-23:25. See if you can begin to answer these questions and put together your own case file of data.

What does the physical evidence reveal about the accused's guilt?
Is there any scientific evidence to substantiate the Prosecution's claims?
Who are the expert witnesses from both sides?
Are they credible? Why or why not?

Bestselling author and Christian apologist Josh McDowell hopes "The New Evidence That Demands a Verdict" will further document historical evidence of the Christian faith.

It is a tool for locating supporting "evidence" whenever the need arises.

Part I addresses the trustworthiness of the Bible;

Part II offers historical evidence and supporting attestations for Jesus' claim to God;

Part III addresses radical Christian criticism of the Bible;

Part IV is devoted to quelling the voice of numerous skeptics, including a defense for the existence of miracles and answers to divergent worldview.[6]

---

[6] http://www.amazon.com/Evidence-Demands-Questions-Challenging-Christians/dp/0785243631

Chapter 4

Is There Probable Cause?

Before our case can get to the Supreme Court, we will summon a Grand Jury to listen to the basic case and evidence and decide if Jesus' appeal should even be heard. If the Grand Jury decides yes, then a trial will follow with the full legal process. For the OJ trial, the Grand Jury was dismissed because of excessive media coverage, so they had a "probable cause" hearing, which a judge presided over and made the decision.

We will follow the OJ protocol and first have a "probable cause" hearing before we try the case of Jesus as the Son of God.

To make matters simple, we will first focus on one foundational issue: *Is there even a God?* If there is no God, then by default, Jesus is guilty, case closed. If there is no God, then Jesus cannot be God's Son. There would be no reason to further explore the validity of the Bible, the impact of biblical prophecy, to learn more about Jesus Christ as God's Son, and to even hear more on the narrative of Christianity. We might be able to end this trial before it starts if you believe there is simply not enough evidence to even prove God exists. If the atheists are right, we can end this proceeding before hearing the evidence of Jesus. You can put this book away and grab some great work of fiction and entertain yourself.

So, you will be the judge for our probable cause hearing. Is there enough evidence for you to believe there is a God? If so, we will proceed with the full trial to consider the claims of Jesus, the Son of God and the resulting claims of Christianity that follow this belief.

The Big Questions

We will let the Dream Team put out their arguments first. All of the great minds of philosophy, science, history, and religion will weigh in as part of the modern day Dream Team in this case. For the first witness, the Dream Team calls, Atheism as the first reason to reject the appeal.

Atheism by definition is the disbelief in the existence of God. Atheists argue there is no solid or tangible evidence for God nor a logical or scientific argument for God. The existence of God is taken on blind faith and not by evidence. The Dream Team argues that God cannot be proven by science which is how we understand our universe and our natural world. It is simply not a fact.

The Dream Team points out there are over 850 Million atheists, so the group that believes this is not small. The atheist camp argues that believing in God is the same as believing in the tooth fairy, the Easter bunny, and Santa Claus. The Christians of Jesus' time were ignorant and did not have science, so this whole notion of God is flawed.

Evolution answers our questions about where we came from so there is no need for a theory of God. There is no tangible proof of God, thus, they cannot believe in God. If there is no God, by logic, there cannot be a son of God. Jesus was then indeed guilty as a blasphemer and by default then, Christianity is a farce.

The Dream Team concludes there is simply no hard proof. Using the standards of logic, we must conclude there is no God, and that means, no need for an appeal or trial on Jesus conviction. A motion is made by the Dream Team to reject the appeal for a new trial on the grounds of Atheism.

The Prosecution argues differently. The brilliant lead lawyer starts the case with a simple rebuttal. God is real. The proof is right in front of us and any reasonable person will conclude, God exists. We will present facts from astronomy, science, and mathematics to convince the judge to proceed with the appeal.

The first exhibit will be Astronomy. How did the universe begin? Recent discoveries in astronomy and physics have shown beyond a reasonable doubt that our universe did in fact have a beginning. So, the first piece entered into evidence is the Bible and specifically, Genesis 1. The biblical account of creation from the Bible states, "In the beginning, God created the Heavens and the Earth. And the earth was formless and void and darkness was over the surface of the deep. Then God said, let there be light and there was light." Continuing on in Genesis, "God created everything in six days. This includes the universe, earth, the mountains and oceans, animals and finally man and then women. After this, he rested on the seventh day. And God saw all that he had made and it was very good."

The Prosecution argues life began when God said so. The universe did not always exist and Science now agrees to this. The best in astronomy, science, and physics all confirm it.

Furthermore, DNA proves the amazing way everything is made, from planets, to animals to the human body. It is unfathomable to believe all of our amazing creation could have happened by chance. The odds confirm it even further, as the mathematicians absolutely conclude this when they consider the probabilities. So, the science community all now agree, everything in the Cosmos started out as a single point in space. In an instant, everything expanded outward from that single location, forming the energy, atoms, and eventually the stars and galaxies we see today.

Was this all just random chance? If things collided, how did the rocks get there to create the Big Bang? From Rocks came human life, animals, planets, oceans, and streams by randomly banging together? Even if you could believe this, then you must ask, where did the matter come from that started it all?

An Expert Witness Changes His Mind

Let's turn to some of the experts to help us. The Prosecution calls its first expert witness, Antony Flew, to the stand. One of the most famous Atheists of all time was Antony Flew, an English philosopher. During the course of his career, he taught at the universities of Oxford, Aberdeen, Keele, Reading, and at York University in Toronto. He also wrote many books. Flew was known as a strong advocate of atheism, arguing that one should presuppose atheism until empirical evidence of a God surfaces. Later in his life in 2004, he shocked the atheist community by changing his mind. The new evidence he found was overwhelming and he had a lifelong commitment to go where the evidence leads. He now believed in the existence of a god. Science provided the proof.

What was the evidence that changed Flew's mind? It was twofold. One big issue that changed his view was the scientific conclusions that came out recently that point to a beginning to our universe. If the universe did have a beginning, by the simple logic, there had to be creator–separate and apart from the effect–that caused it. If there was a creator who had the power and glory to create this, does this fit the description of the God of the Bible? Does it fit the narrative of the Bible? By all accounts, it does.

Author Eric Metaxas in his book "Miracles," cites the amazing summary of the scientific factors required for life on earth and longshot odds of this all occurring. The Prosecution enters this book into evidence as a must read for the science minded seeker to consider.

The book relates details around the amazing odds of earth emerging randomly from the Big Bang and being able to sustain life. The odds are mind boggling, given there has to be an estimated 150 factors in place for a planet to support life such as the size of the earth. If earth was slightly larger, it would have more gravity and the atmosphere would then have too much methane and Ammonia that we could not breathe. If the earth was slightly smaller, we would have less gravity and then water would evaporate and we would not be able to sustain life. It took precision at the highest level for us to exist and live on this planet.

Another example Metaxas cites in his book is the presence of a large planet in our universe, Jupiter, which is 122 times the size of earth. The gravity of Jupiter, because of its size, attracts most of the comets the come anywhere near Jupiter, keeping earth safe. Without Jupiter, the earth would be pummeled by asteroids and meteors and not exist as it does today.

Another amazing fact that sustains life as we know it on earth is our Moon. Interestingly, Earth is the only planet in the universe with one moon. The belief from science is that a big collision with our earth perfectly caused our moon. This then created the stable force of gravity that keeps our earth tilt perfect for life, ocean tides, and weather. Without our single moon exactly where it sits in relation to the earth, there would be no life on earth. For some reason, earth is the only plant in our universe with one single moon. Pure chance or intelligent design?

When the experts calculate the odds of a perfect set of circumstances necessary for life on a planet which are in place for earth, the odds are one expressed visually in Eric Metaxas book as 1 in 100,000,000,000,000,000,000,000,000,000,000,000,000,000,000.

The arguments on intelligent design actually go on and on and on, but we must ask, "Is Earth and life as we know it all chance, making us the most amazing statistic in the history of mathematics or are we the result of a very powerful and intelligent creator? One in a trillion chance? Did we just beat the odds and it's all random or there is a higher power?"

Closing Arguments in the God Phase of the Trial

So in closing out this first leg of the argument, the scientific experts for the Dream Team assert that we cannot know how the universe was created, and we have no proof, so there can be no God. They also argue that the earth, the universe, and the entire human race were all created by chance. The Big Bang theory experts basically assert a random chance event, where the planets collided and magically the planets, stars, earth, animals, people, and food all just appeared. We beat the most amazing odds ever in order to be alive and breathing here on the Earth. Thus, no God and no need for a retrial, case closed.

Dr. John Lennox, Professor of Mathematics at Oxford University and an internationally renowned speaker on the interface of science, philosophy, and religion, writes, "There are not many options—essentially just two. Either human intelligence ultimately owes its origin to mindless matter; or there is a Creator. It is strange that some people claim that it is their intelligence that leads them to prefer the first to the second." If you prefer to look at the odds and consider the two choices, the answer seems to clearly point to God.

Evolution versus Creation and Intelligent Design

The Dream Team now calls to the stand, Charles Darwin, and the theory of Evolution. Scientists assert that over time, things changed, things happened, and simple organisms become more complex. Things grew from cells to creatures to animals to chimpanzees to apes to humans. From rocks in space with no life form to human life. It was all pure dumb luck. Planets collided and here we are living with complex brains, amazing human bodies, life giving hearts, emotions, and feelings.

Even if you think the rocks colliding randomly theory makes sense, then the next big leap you have to make is atheists believe that evolution occurred. Darwin argues that over millions of years, successive generations of genetic variations gave survival enhancements and brought about new species. The theory is that thousands of generations of small changes resulted in a species that can look very different from the one that it came from and the fit will survive while the weak will die and wither. Some seemingly smart scientists argue this is the case and believe the Big Bang, then gradual evolution, and no God.

The Prosecution begins the argument with a simple statement. No one can prove the theory of evolution. It is a theory.

We will just touch the surface of this argument by saying Intelligent Design versus Evolution makes more sense. The Intelligent Design movement promotes the idea that many aspects of life are too complex to have evolved without the intervention of a supernatural being—the intelligent designer, God.

Antony Flew was swayed from Atheism on a second fact. He was overwhelmed by the complexity of our design. In a recording of the 2004 symposium "Has Science Discovered God," organized by *The Institute for Metascientific Research,* Professor Flew says: "What I think the DNA material has done is show that intelligence must have been involved in getting these extraordinarily diverse elements together. The enormous complexity by which the results were achieved look to me like the work of intelligence."

The Prosecution calls Science to the stand to talk about DNA.

DNA is a molecule that contains our unique genetic code. Like a recipe book, it holds the instructions for making all the proteins in our bodies. DNA in our cells is very similar to a complex computer program. Computer programs are made up of a series of ones and zeros, called binary code. That's the language of programming for machines of today. The sequencing and ordering of these ones and zeros is what makes the computer program work properly. Computers can do amazingly complex things in seconds. Our most powerful computer could arguably be the Cray Titan Supercomputer. This amazing computer uses 18,688 CPUs paired with an equal number of GPUs to perform at a theoretical peak of twenty-seven petaFLOPS, unfathomable power by computer standards. It is estimated this supercomputer costs close to $100 Million dollars.

Compared to the code in the Cray supercomputer, the DNA System is even more amazingly designed and complex. In the same way a supercomputer processes zeros and ones, DNA is the body's complex computer code but even more robust. DNA is made up of four chemicals, abbreviated as letters A, T, G, and C. Much like the ones and zeros in the Titan Supecomputer, these letters are arranged in the human cell like this: CGTGTGACTCGCTCCTGAT and so on. The order in which they are arranged instructs the cell's actions and creates our individual nuances of looks, body size, and brains.

Where this gets a bit mind-bending is in the complexity. Within the tiny space in every cell in your body, this DNA code is **three billion letters long**. Every single Cell = 3 Billion letters. It is estimated there are 37 trillion cells in our bodies.

So, stepping back, to grasp the amount of DNA information in one cell, if you were to do a live reading of the DNA code at a rate of three letters per second, it would take thirty-one years to read the code in one cell, even if reading continued day and night.

On top of this, it has been determined that 99.9 percent of your DNA is similar to everyone's genetic makeup. What is uniquely *you* comes in the fractional difference in how those three billion letters are sequenced in your cells. The U.S. government is able to identify everyone in our country by the arrangement of a nine-digit social security numbers. Yet, inside every cell in you is a three-billion-lettered DNA structure that belongs only to you. This code identifies you and continually instructs your cells' behavior. It defines who you are as a unique human being, from looks, intelligence, and physical traits.

If you put all the DNA molecules in your body end to end, the DNA would reach from the Earth to the Sun and back over 600 times.

To add celebrity flavor to the argument, the Prosecution calls former President Bill Clinton to the stand to provide one person's insight into the DNA evidence. On June 26, 2000, President Clinton congratulated those who completed the famous human genome sequencing project saying, "Today we are learning the language in which God created life. We are gaining ever more awe for the complexity, the beauty, the wonder of God's most divine and sacred gift." Dr. Francis Collins, director of the Human Genome Project, followed Clinton to the podium stating, "It is humbling for me and awe inspiring to realize that we have caught the first glimpse of our own instruction book, previously known only to God."

When looking at the DNA structure within the human body, we cannot escape the presence of incredibly intelligent design. A code that is beyond our understanding, one so complex we can only venture to guess how the code is written, organized, and brought to life.

While DNA is amazing in itself, the simple beauty of our universe, and the vast number of planets and stars is mind boggling. If we look as just the earth in a recent count, there are over 7.77 million animal species and 300,000 plant species.

Closing Arguments

In closing, the Dream Team, argues there is no God. This is all the result of a random Big Bang Theory. Out of nothing, came life, and evolution. From simple rocks and amoebas came our complex world, planets, and our amazing bodies. God does not exist, he has never existed and thus, the case should be dismissed. No god, no unjust conviction of his son.

The Prosecution will focus on the closing comments on the odds, looking at mathematics and statistics. What are the chances of a Rolex watch with over 115 separate parts just assembling itself and creating a Rolex? They are amazing timepieces with so many intricate pieces. Could that just happen? How about one of the marvels of the air, the Boeing 777 with three million separate parts assemble itself? Could rocks collide and bam, we have Rolex and a Boeing 777? Maybe a jet would evolve over a billion years on its own.

Our world, our bodies, our universe are much more complex than any watch or jumbo jet and much less likely to have randomly appeared and assembled then a Rolex watch. It is statistically more probably we would find a jumbo jet assembled than our universe and human life appearing from nothing.

How could it be that our life sustaining Earth, with expert handicapped odds of 1–100 billion, just appeared and beat the odds? Once we did that, what about life and design? From nothing came something? From rocks came living beings and amazing DNA that makes us all who we are and who we are not? Our human bodies evolved from some single cell that divided and turned into hands, feet, brains, hearts, and minds?

Or does it makes more sense that an amazingly complex, powerful, and intelligent God created this world versus the belief that this is all the result of a random collision that from nothing, came everything?

The Prosecution argues the existence of God is not just likely, but it is the only explanation that a reasonable person would be able to conclude from the evidence that has been left for us to see. The odds drive the decision to certainty. The Prosecution rests its case.

Dig in and Examine What the Facts Tell Us

As the judge in this preliminary hearing, ask yourself:

Did humans defy all the odds by evolving from cosmic rocks into cells, into animals, into amazingly complex humans?

Or is it all the result of an amazing designer, a God, who made everything you see, you touch, and you feel?
Do we have probable cause to believe God exists?
Should Jesus' appeal be heard?

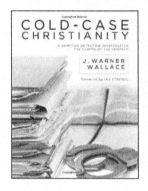 *Written by an L. A. County homicide detective and former atheist, Cold-Case Christianity examines the claims of the New Testament using the skills and strategies of a hard-to-convince criminal investigator.* Christianity could be defined as a "cold case": it makes a claim about an event from the distant past for which there is little forensic evidence. In Cold-Case Christianity, J. Warner Wallace uses his nationally recognized skills as a homicide detective to look at the evidence and eyewitnesses behind Christian beliefs.[7]

---

[7] www.coldcasechristianity.com

Chapter 5

Motive and Timeline

Like the OJ case, a good place to start will be with a basic motive and timeline. One of the most compelling in the OJ case was the entire narrative of his relationship with Nicole Brown, which led to motive being very clear. The timeline of that day left no doubt he had the window of time to commit the murder and there was no alibi or conflict that would say OJ was innocent. His rocky relationship and history of violence and jealousy could lead a juror to clearly see the story of what happened. The timeline and the motive alone could have convinced many of his guilt.

What about in our trial?
What is God's overall motive in all this?
Why would God, creator of the universe send his son to Earth and change the system?
Does the Bible timeline fit the Jesus narrative?

The Biblical Narrative

The Bible lays out a grand narrative of God and Christianity contending God created the heavens and earth. After God created Adam and Eve, we are told of the fall of man to sin as Adam and Eve disobeyed God. They were then separated from God by sin, however, God had a master plan to send a Messiah, his own Son, Jesus Christ into the world, to show his love for us and change everything.

In the Old Testament, God gave man the roadmap and rule book for holy living. Man continually failed from the time of Adam to Christ's death, to live according to the holy requirements of God, with sin being rampant and every human falling short of being able to live the perfect holy life God initially planned for Adam and Eve.

God Sends His Son

By sending Jesus, his own Son, God would teach us many things about his character, his priorities, and his plans for us. Jesus was God living with us on Earth. He would show us what love was, and then in the most unselfish act, allow his Son to die a criminal's death as a sacrifice to wash away our flaws and sins and open the door to an eternal relationship with him. It was a salvation we could not earn, but a free gift from God.

The essence of Christianity is following Christ as God's Son and his teachings. When Christ died, later rose from the dead and appeared to hundreds of people, a multitude of biblical prophecies written hundreds of years before his arrival were fulfilled. His death and resurrection changed everything causing his followers to start the Christianity movement. Simple faith in Jesus Christ leads to a relationship with God, salvation, and eternal life. That's the story. Now we have to determine if the timeline from Genesis to Jesus' resurrection fits the claims.

Here is a basic timeline of creation to Christ's birth as told in the Bible:

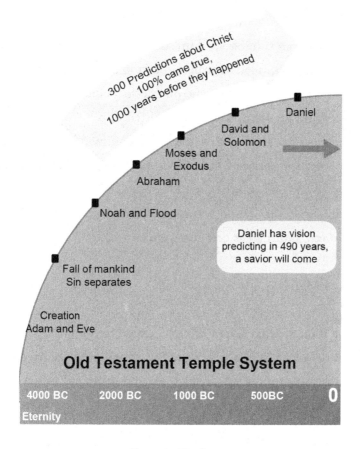

Temple System
Sin – Sacrifice

- 613 Rules
- 10 Commandments
- How to worship
- How to atone
- How to live and be distinct

Creation

Genesis, the first book of the Bible, tells of creation and how everything came because of a creator. According to Genesis, God created mankind in his own image. That is an interesting glimpse into God. We also see that God said, "It is not good for the man to be alone; I will make him a helper suitable for him so he created Eve, his companion. For this reason a man shall leave his father and his mother, and be joined to his wife; and they shall become one flesh."[8] God created the beauty of marriage and of a man and a women that day.

In this new world, God gave them one commandment, "From any tree of the garden you may eat freely; but from the tree of the knowledge of good and evil you shall not eat, for in the day that you eat from it you will surely die."[9] God was with man before the fall, they lived together; God and man as one community.

The Fall of Man

As we look at what happens next, a big concept you will need to wrestle with is Free Will. God created us all with the ability to choose. He did not want robots who had to worship him and follow him, he wanted us all to make a choice to believe, follow, and love him. Adam was on earth, without sin, but God had given him a will which gave Adam the potential to sin. It was his choice just like all of us. God does not force us to believe in him, worship him or follow his teachings. The Bible goes on to then report that a serpent, wiser and craftier than all

---

[8] Genesis 2:18, 20b-25

[9] Genesis 2:15-17

others, tempted Eve and told her she should try the forbidden fruit for surely she will not die. Eve brought the fruit to Adam and they ate the fruit, disobeying God.[10]

In Ezekiel 28:12-17, the Bible gives us information concerning Satan, also known as the serpent. He was likely the highest of all the angels in heaven and the most beautiful. His heart became proud because of his beauty and he became evil. He wanted to be above God and determined to set up his own throne that men might worship him. Satan led a rebellion in heaven against God and then proceeded to tempt man also to disobey God. Adam and Eve, having sinned by disobeying God, had broken intimate fellowship with God.

So we entered a period where there was a new way God communicated to the people, through laws, rules, and through his prophets like Moses and Isaiah. The Old Testament of the Bible and the Torah recorded what happened through these amazing times on earth. The stories were told of many generations having the choice to follow God or live in sin. Man, with a flawed nature, continued to disappoint God. The pattern was not good. Through the stories of Noah and the flood, Sodom and Gomorrah, wars and disputes, Jonah and the whale, and more, we read stories of pain and suffering due to sin and not following God's plans and guidelines.

Moses was given the Ten Commandments directly from God to help guide the Jewish people on how to live following godly principles. Dennis Praeger explains it eloquently on his website at Praeger University, "Humanity has everything it needs to create a good world. We've had it for 3,000 years. It's the Ten Commandments—ten basic, yet profound instructions for how to lead a moral life. If everyone followed the Ten

---

[10] Genesis 3:1-6

Commandments, we would not need armies or police; marriages and families would be stronger; truth would be a paramount value."

We can look in the book of Exodus 20 for the list of the rules and regulations God provided to us:

1) "You shall have no other gods before me.
2) You shall not make for yourself an image in the form of anything in heaven above or on the earth beneath or in the waters below. You shall not bow down to them or worship them; for I, the Lord your God, am a jealous God, punishing the children for the sin of the parents to the third and fourth generation of those who hate me, but showing love to a thousand generations of those who love me and keep my commandments.
3) You shall not misuse the name of the Lord your God, for the Lord will not hold anyone guiltless who misuses his name.
4) Remember the Sabbath day by keeping it holy. Six days you shall labor and do all your work, but the seventh day is a Sabbath to the Lord your God. On it you shall not do any work, neither you, nor your son or daughter, nor your male or female servant, nor your animals, nor any foreigner residing in your towns. For in six days the Lord made the heavens and the earth, the sea, and all that is in them, but he rested on the seventh day. Therefore the Lord blessed the Sabbath day and made it holy.
5) Honor your father and your mother, so that you may live long in the land the Lord your God is giving you.
6) You shall not murder.
7) You shall not commit adultery.
8) You shall not steal.
9) You shall not give false testimony against your neighbor.

10) You shall not covet your neighbor's house. You shall not covet your neighbor's wife, or his male or female servant, his ox or donkey, or anything that belongs to your neighbor."

As time went on, these ten were expanded by Old Testament generations to include 600 even more specific rules or guidelines that would lay out the way godly people should live, worship, and treat each other. Some call this the temple system, where you would follow rules, certain rituals, and make sacrifices to be holy enough to be close to God. Many rules existed around what you could eat to remain holy, how you acted and dressed, and if you sinned, how to atone and make sacrifices of blood. The temple system had several types of sacrifices people would make to God for different reasons. A burnt offering was to show love for God. A grain and the peace offerings were geared to reconciliation and peace. A sin offering was for specific sins committed. The Book of Leviticus in the Old Testament lays out the complex and onerous system. Blood would wash away the sin before Christ. That's how God set it up and this set the table for Christ's blood later.

With this, God watched his people and provided wisdom through the prophets such as Abraham, Moses, and Isaiah. This was a "rules based" time, with lots of guidelines provided as a guide to daily living and communion with God. Sacrifices to God as worship and thanks were part of the system. It started with Adam and continued through Christ, until Christ's blood was shed to change it all.

God's power and might are shown through King David, through the wisdom and wealth of King Solomon, and through mighty battles where God's strength prevailed over man. A fascinating time in world history can be studied through the accounts recorded in the Old Testament.

Warning: Plot Twist

However, this is where the story gets very interesting, so pay attention. Throughout this 2000-3000 year period before Christ's birth, God revealed the change that was coming through his prophets. The temple system with sacrifices and rules would be replaced by the one and only Messiah, a savior who would change the game for all of us and provide the path to eternal life and forgiveness of our sins. It was to be one big sacrifice for all sins. A loving gift like no other.

This is where the statisticians will have a field day. In the Old Testament there were over 300 prophecies or predictions about the coming Messiah, hundreds of years before Christ came. Amazing prophecies about Christ's arrival and life including where and when he would be born, how he would die, where he would live, and what he would do.

100 percent of the Old Testament prophecies came true in Jesus.

The odds of 300+ prophecies coming true that were given 500 years before Christ was even born are beyond mathematical probability! The odds are off the charts and many doubters have changed their view when they look at this closely. As predicted, Jesus was born and a new and amazing paradigm shift occurred. Jesus changed everything. Not only did he die, he then rose from the dead. Death had no power over God's Son, Jesus Christ just as the prophecies 500 years before had predicted. Amazing!

Motive and Timeline

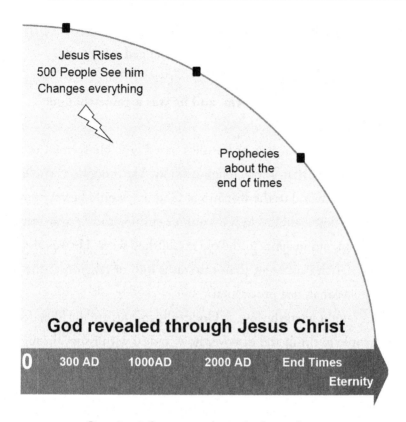

Greatest Commandments from Jesus
- Love God with all your Heart
- Love your neighbor as yourself

Salvation through Faith, not works

What Actual Did Jesus Teach and Say?

Jesus began his ministry when he was thirty years old. He started with amazing miracles, from healings to bringing the dead back to life. Along the way, Jesus assembled a small team to follow him, called his disciples. His disciples were not holy men or highly educated men of the time, but common folks like fishermen and tax collectors. His period of time teaching was just 3 ½ years, but it changed everything.

Jesus was God in human form, and he was a game changer

Surprisingly, Jesus was not a rules based guy. He seemed to shun organized, holier than thou, religious piety. He brought a whole new mindset to faith and to the worship of God. He would be very popular today with these beliefs. He was counter culture and he was bringing new wisdom and insights to the old established ways. He was also very controversial and different than the status quo of religion at the time. He was relational, not procedural.

Jesus taught what the love of God really meant, and he liked to challenge people to think and discover how to deal with issues through his parables and stories. His teaching style was a game changer. One two-part fundamental principle really embodied the new message of Christ.

Commandment one: Love God with all your heart, mind, and soul
Commandment two: Love your neighbor as yourself[1]

He shared a powerful and paradigm shifting story in the parable of the Good Samaritan saying God calls us to care and love those in need, those less fortunate, and those who need a helping hand. Jesus showed clear disdain for self-righteous, hypocritical, judgmental, religious leaders, and he chose to hang out and teach those society hated including tax collectors, prostitutes, and various well known society sinners. The religious leaders of the day rejected him and his messages.

---

[11] We find this account in Matthew 22: 36-40, when Jesus was asked by a wise lawyer what the greatest commandment was.

They did not see him as the great Messiah predicted 500 years before even though he fit the criteria by performing amazing miracles and bringing a new message of love. They were blinded to who he was, God's Son, who had come to change everything.

A quick read through the Book of John will give you a glimpse into the life of Christ and his teachings. He modeled love in a way that had never been seen before that was truly amazing.

Besides the message of love, Jesus taught there is eternal life available with God only through him,[12] he made sure we all knew there is clearly good and evil, and there is an evil one that was powerful and is out to ruin us. Even while he was being crucified on the cross, one of the two criminals on the cross believed Jesus was truly God's Son.

Jesus Death and Resurrection

As predicted clearly in the Bible, all of the details of detailed prophecies of his crucifixion and death came true. This was God's plan and Jesus knew what was coming. This was his purpose. As predicted, Jesus was betrayed by one of his own, apprehended, and tried for the claims of alleging he was God's Son. He did not refute the claims made against him. He did not recount under pressure of death. He was sentenced to death on a cross, which he accepted. It was God's plan. Our sin would be washed away forever by his Son and this gift he gave us. No greater love does one have then to lay their life down for another. Jesus did that for us.

Jesus also fulfilled the Old Testament prophecies that predicted how the soldiers would gamble for his clothing, how a rich man's tomb

---

[12] See John 3:16 and 14:6

would be where he was laid to rest, and the exact details about how his hands and feet would be pierced, yet he would not have a single broken bone. Amazing prophecies about minute details, that all came true in Christ. The most important part of this story is that Jesus did not just die, he rose from the dead on the third day as the Bible predicted and he was then seen by over 500 people in his resurrected body.

The twelve disciples, who seemed confused and depressed after his death, changed from sad, cowardly fisherman and tax collectors, who were privately lamenting the death of Christ, to zealous and on fire witnesses who would go to the ends of the earth telling everyone what they saw and willing to die instead of denying the truth they witnessed in an amazing way. This was the last straw of transformation for the faith in Jesus and the emergence of the Jesus followers, who became the first generation of Christians.

Christ revealed himself in his resurrected body and the amazing story was complete! No longer did we need the temple system to get to God, it was simple, as Jesus taught.

Faith alone was the route to God, not works or sacrifices. We can't earn it, we don't deserve it, it is a free gift, but it takes belief and then acceptance. It takes faith. The religiosity of doing the right thing was replaced with love and a simple message.

God provides us with plenty of proof to confidently believe. It became so simple, so clear, and so predicted! How could anyone disagree with the joy in Christ's teachings, the amazing connection to prophecy, and the connection to the timelines of God as he revealed to us through his word.

Closing out the Timeline

So, what's next, how does the timeline play out? The Bible teaches that this earth will end and then God will restore Heaven on Earth. The apostle John in the Book of Revelation gives us amazing predictions about the end times and the warning signs to look for since our earth does have an expiration date. The vision of the last days made 2000+ years ago are an amazing additional proof of the power of God. The Bible teaches these signs of a coming end times that must be fulfilled:

1. Worldwide Breakdown of Character
2. False Christianity Prevalent
3. Wars and Unrest Grow Much Worst
4. Famines
5. Deadly Disease
6. Earthquakes and Volcanic Activity
7. The Gospel would be Preached to the Entire World
8. A United Europe
9. A World Leader Emerges
10. One World Government
11. One World Currency

Given the Bible's track record of accuracy in prophecy and predictions, it is hard to dispute what will ultimately be coming for life on Earth. A study of the biblical prophecies of the end times could be enough to convince many of God's existence and the validity of the Bible alone. It is truly amazing what was predicted 2500 years ago about how people would not be able to buy or sell anything without a "mark" or chip that tracked everything, about a one world government, and about how the Middle East and Israel will play a part in this final chapter. The internet, communications, and our financial markets have progressed to where literally every circumstance needed for the final fulfillment seems possible now. They were not possible 100 years ago, but today the infrastructure is in place and the stage is set.

So, this is the Christian narrative as told in the Bible, starting with Adam and Eve and creation and ending with the end of earth and final judgement. At the center of the story is Jesus Christ who was predicted years before he came and worshiped thousands of years after he arose.

Truly the most amazing and impactful person in the history of the world.

So Did Jesus Even Exist? Can We Prove it?

It's time to dig back into the case and hear the arguments on both sides so we can consider this thoughtfully together.

The Dream Team decides to register an objection. How can you prove Jesus if your only source is the Bible, which we don't yet accept as credible? If you take the Bible out as evidence, then what do you have to say this man even existed?

The Prosecution responds. There is tremendous proof of Jesus' existence outside of the Bible. The Prosecution enters into evidence, J. Warner Wallace book "Cold Case Christianity" where he sums up the non-biblical accounts of Jesus, which are highlighted from eleven different sources over the years after Jesus death.

What would we know about Jesus if we lost every possible Christian document including the New Testament and writings of the church fathers? What would the earliest unfriendly Greek, Roman, Syrian, and Jewish historical documents tell us about Jesus?

- *Jesus was born and lived in Palestine.*

- *He was born to a woman named Mary and his father was Joseph who was a carpenter.*
- *He was a teacher who taught repentance and godly love for one another.*
- *He led the Jews away from their works focused beliefs.*
- *He was a wise man who claimed to be God and the Messiah.*
- *He had unusual magical powers and performed miraculous deeds.*
- *He healed the lame and accurately predicted the future.*
- *He was persecuted by the Jews for what He said and betrayed by Judas.*
- *He was beaten with rods, forced to drink vinegar, and wear a crown of thorns.*
- *He was crucified on the eve of the Passover.*
- *Crucifixion occurred under the direction of Pontius Pilate, during the time of Tiberius.*
- *On the day of His crucifixion, the sky grew dark and there was an earthquake.*
- *Afterward, He was buried in a tomb that was later found to be empty.*
- *He appeared to His disciples resurrected from the grave and showed them His wounds.*
- *These disciples then told others Jesus was resurrected and ascended into heaven.*
- *Jesus' disciples and followers upheld a high moral code.*
- *One of them was named Matthew and another was a doctor named Luke.*
- *His disciples were persecuted and martyred for their faith without changing their claims.*
- *They met regularly to worship Jesus, even after His death.*

The sources of this information include a well-known historian, Josephus (37-101 A.D.), who was a historian to Jewish Rabbis. Thallus was another, who wrote in 52 A.D., who as a secular writer. Tacitus, an ancient historian who lived in 56 A.D.-120 A.D. was a trusted ancient historian, and there were many more.

Concluding the historical proof of Jesus, the Prosecution says, "Despite the enormous range of opinion, there are several points on which virtually all scholars of antiquity agree. Jesus was a Jewish man, known to be a preacher and teacher, who was crucified (a Roman form of execution) in Jerusalem during the reign of the Roman emperor Tiberius, when Pontius Pilate was the governor of Judea."

The Dream Team rises to the podium, "We will enter into the record, Jesus did exist based on this evidence, but beyond that we have many questions. Jesus was a wonderful man, truly a great teacher, a thinker of his time, maybe even a prophet or one of many messengers from God, but beyond that, we don't know. Surely a man of history and innovative thinking. One of the great ones for sure, but we cannot agree that he was God's Son."

The Prosecution pauses to counter this argument head on. Rising slowly to the stand, the lead attorney slowly states, "Either Jesus Christ was who he claimed to be, the Son of God, or he was the biggest fraud and con man in the history of the world. He claimed to be God's Son, he claimed to heal the sick, raise the dead, and forgive sins. He claimed to be the only way to God and Heaven. He was who he said he was or he was a hoax. There is no middle ground."

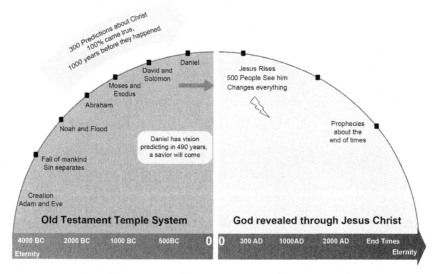

Temple System
Sin – Sacrifice
- 613 Rules
- 10 Commandments
- How to worship
- How to atone
- How to live and be distinct

Greatest Commandments from Jesus
- Love God with all your Heart
- Love your neighbor as yourself

Salvation through Faith, not works

Dig in and Examine What the Facts Tell Us

Like the OJ case, the timeline and motive matter.
So, reviewing the timeline, motive, and overall narrative, does the story fit?
Does it make sense when you consider all of God's plan for us?
Did Jesus actually exist or is this all a big myth like Big Foot?
If he existed, was he merely a delusional con man or truly the Messiah, God's Son?
How did God tell us what was coming?
How many of these prophecies came true?

 As a young man, Josh McDowell considered himself an agnostic. He truly believed that Christianity was worthless. However, when challenged to intellectually examine the claims of Christianity, Josh discovered compelling, overwhelming evidence for the reliability of the Christian faith. In 1961 Josh joined the staff of Campus Crusade for Christ International. Not long after, he started the Josh McDowell Ministry to reach young people worldwide with the truth and love of Jesus.

He writes, "Although it was first written on perishable materials, and had to be copied and recopied for hundreds of years before the invention of the printing press, the Scriptures have never diminished in style or correctness, nor have they ever faced extinction. Compared with other ancient writings, the Bible has more manuscript evidence to support it than any ten pieces of classical literature combined."[13]

---

[13] http://www.christianbook.com/bible-really-dialogue-skepticism-evidence-truth/josh-mcdowell/9780802487667/pd/487667

Chapter 6

The Bible: Admit to Evidence or Unreliable?

If the Bible is not reliable and God inspired, then all this faith stuff falls very short. We need to spend some time considering whether we can rely on the Bible in this case.

Christians regard the Bible as God's written message to humankind. In addition to being the historical record of Jesus' life and miracles, the Bible reveals God's personality, his love, truth, and how we can have a relationship with him.

Hundreds of millions of people's faith rests on the teachings contained in the Bible. Many do so unquestioningly. For the inquiring and skeptical mind, blind belief in the authenticity of the Bible is not good enough. For our case, we need to show the Bible is from God and its message has not changed over time. The good news is there is a tremendous amount of quality research that has gone into this subject to help answer some of the questions about God's Word.

Is the Bible True and God's Word?

The Dream Team opens this part of the trial with a cutting and thought provoking opening statement. "You're referring to a book that was written by men, edited by men, and published by men. Yet you, and so many others refer to it as God's Word. Talk about ignorance or is it stupidity? We cannot consider this book as evidence as God's Word. There is no proof to support that claim. It's just a history book written by regular humans, no more."

The Dream Team further asserts the Bible is a historically unreliable collection of legends or myths. A best seller for sure, but fiction in the genre of a Steven King novel or the Harry Potter series.

"Additionally," the Dream Team emphasizes, "It was written and then translated many times over and cannot even be considered accurate. History does not prove out many things that were cited in the Bible so how can mere human words be the basis for what Christians cling to as their holy book? The parting of the Red Sea, Noah and the Ark, Jonah and the Whale are tales great for children's stories, but we are an enlightened generation so we must discount these as mere fictional stories of the day. If you take out the Bible, the stories, and the prophecies, the case for Jesus being God's Son crumbles."

So, what about this book called the Bible?

The Prosecution responds with confidence and with passion, "To set the record straight, let's clarify for the court what the Bible is so we have a clear understanding. Although it is impossible to obtain exact figures, there is little doubt that the Bible is the world's best-selling and most widely distributed book. A survey by the Bible Society concluded that around 2.5 billion copies were printed between 1815 and 1975 alone, but more recent estimates put the number at more than 5 billion. Charles Dickens, *A Tale of Two Cities* is in a close second position with 200 Million copies, a mere 4.8 Billion copies behind the Bible."

The Bible was written over a period about 1500 years by forty different authors. These authors ranged from kings, peasants, philosophers, fishermen, historians, doctors, poets, and scholars. The sixty-six books were written in three languages. The Old Testament in Hebrew, some Aramaic and Greek for the New Testament.

It is clearly the most historically preserved and documented book in history with over 1000 old original manuscripts verifying the accuracy. The book survived much persecution through the centuries from the Romans to Hitler banning the book and many other historical challenges to God's Word.

The modern Bible is broken into two parts: The Old Testament and the New Testament. The Old Testament is the thirty-nine books written before Christ. It is the basis of Judaism and faith, from Genesis to Moses and the Exodus, and on to the amazing Psalms and Proverbs of David.

The New Testament, which is made up of twenty-seven books includes the Gospels that tell of Jesus' life on earth. The four gospels, Matthew, Mark, Luke, and John are all direct reports on Jesus' life and teachings, three from those who lived with Christ. The fourth, Luke, is from the view of a historian, who recapped the story after much research and interviewing witnesses. The Gospels form the meat and potatoes of the Christian faith and Jesus' direct teachings to the world.

So, how did all these books and writing end up as the book we now call the Bible? In about 300 A.D., the Christian church spent considerable time reviewing which New Testament books should be included in the Bible, based on author, the accuracy, and timespans written from the events occurring. This led to the selection of the books we now call the Bible.

"The Dream Team could assert this was man's work, not God's, so the selection is flawed," observes the Prosecution. "However, the consistency and accuracy of the stories, verified by historical accounts brings credibility to the argument. Secondly, if God is powerful enough to create everything, then inspiring the writings and helping a team know which ones to select would certainly be a very simple task for a powerful and divine God. As a book, the Bible has no equal. It is simply the most amazing book ever written by any account."

Science and the Bible's Claims

Can we find other ways to prove the Bible is no ordinary book? We should look at this closely for sure. Interestingly, nothing in science contradicts the writings in the Bible, which is amazing in itself. In the book of Genesis, written at least 3500 years ago, it talks about the order of creation, from universe to earth, the life in the oceans, then life on land, and finally, human beings. This specific order of life was confirmed by science in our lifetime, but how could this have been known back then? A lucky guess? A crazy coincidence?

The Bible is full of amazing scientific statements that were recorded many centuries before men discovered them. For example, the Bible said the earth was round when men said it was flat (Isaiah 40:22); man wouldn't discover this until 2,600 years later! In an age when men thought the earth sat on the back of a large animal, the Bible recorded that the earth floated in empty space (Job 26:7). The Bible describes the cycle of air currents a couple thousand years before men discovered them (Ecclesiastes 1:6). Jesus said His Second Coming would occur when some are awake working in a field and others are asleep in their beds, describing the rotation of the earth before it was ever discovered by men (Luke 17:34-36). There are many more amazing scientific facts in the Bible. Oddly, 100 percent were accurate before telescopes and carbon dating. Dumb luck or something more divine? Why were there no mistakes in these writing about scientific facts?

The Bible Is Historically Flawless

Pundits, including the Dream Team, assert the Bible is simply not historically accurate or proven. However, upon closer examination, this is simply not true. The Bible is a flawless historical document. From the order of Kings who ruled during those days to the actual descriptive kingdoms, the Bible is an amazing historical book outlining what happened over the past 4000 years. The Bible accurately and historically recounts the specific order of forty kings living from 2000 BC to 400 BC in exact order, which is supported outside the Bible by reams of historical evidence. Mathematicians estimate the odds of this being random and accurate at 750 trillion to 1. Oddly, the Bible and history agree. More dumb luck or is the Bible getting your attention?

Nothing in the historical or archeological records refutes what the bible says

Yes, we hear claims from time to time that arise that have the one flaw that discounts the whole Bible and God. One recent such claim made by the pundits involved the existence of a group of people called the Hittites that existed thousands of years ago, according to the Bible.

The Bible relates stories about King David killing a soldier, Uriah, who was a Hittite. There were lots of references to this group of people in Bible, but there seemed to be no historical proof they even existed. The pundits pounded on this as the smoking gun claiming they found the glitch.

This doubt, like all others previously raised, was erased recently when an amazing discovery occurred in Turkey that uncovered a big storage room with ten thousand clay tablets. The finding confirmed the existence of the ancient society, the Hittites, adding another feather in the perfect track record the Bible has in accuracy.

What about Archeology?

In "Archaeology Confirms 50 Real People in the Bible" in the March/April 2014 issue of *Biblical Archaeology Review* (**BAR**), Purdue University scholar, Lawrence Mykytiuk, lists fifty figures from the Hebrew Bible who have been confirmed archaeologically. The 50-person chart in **BAR** includes Israelite kings and Mesopotamian monarchs as well as lesser-known figures. Mykytiuk writes, "At least 50 people mentioned in the Bible have been identified in the archaeological records. Their names appear in inscriptions written during the period described by the Bible and in most instances during or quite close to the lifetime of the person identified." The extensive biblical and archaeological documentation supporting the **BAR** study is a great place for a skeptic to research and to see how accurate the Bible was using Archaeology as the measuring stick.

Flipping this argument on its head to look at this differently, there is no reliable historical evidence contrary to what the Bible claims. No historical proof creates problems for the accuracy of the Bible. New

Testament key figures such as John the Baptist, Jesus of Nazareth, and James the leader of the Jerusalem church, have all been mentioned in Jewish and secular history texts as having actually existed as real people, outside the claims of the Bible.

Did the Bible change over time and get diluted over 2000 years?

The Dream Team asserts a simple fact around the Bible. A story or legend changes over time, like the myth of the Loch Ness Monster or Big foot. 500 years later, a tale could become a fact and get distorted with new details and embellishments. With this logic, they can assert that maybe the Bible was changed over time, the story evolved and turned into a bigger legend as one generation told it to the next. After all, it was hand written and then re-written many times, it must have evolved. It must have been embellished as the stories were told about what happened and what was written has certainly changed. Like a children's game of telephone, where a story is whispered into one person's ear and told around the circle until it returns as a completely new version, the accounts of God must have been through this same humanly flawed process.

The Prosecution winces a bit and considers this statement before responding. While this seems like a sound argument to discredit the Bible, the reality is it didn't happen this way! The proof came in 1948. Two shepherd boys in Palestine were exploring some hidden caves in the countryside. While doing this, they made an amazing discovery of some old pottery jars in a hidden cave. Experts converged to see what was found and the findings were truly amazing. The two boys found ancient documents that were 2000 years old and had been untouched for twenty centuries, locked away in this hidden cave until that day. The scrolls, called the famous Dead Sea Scrolls, contained the book of Isaiah from the Old Testament.

Maybe this was the smoking gun to prove the massive changes in the Bible over time. Surely, this would set the record straight. Things must have changed from the original to the current Bible and this would prove it. Except it didn't. It confirmed and provided the evidence that the one and only Bible was the same today, as it was 2000 years ago in the book of Isaiah. The accuracy from that hand written version 2000 years ago to today's Bible was off the charts accurate. The text did not change or morph and the stories were the same.

The final proof the Bible is God's Word

While these are all compelling arguments to the historical accuracy and uniqueness of the Bible, there is more that takes this argument off the charts. The proof is prophecy.

Prophecy in the Bible is the final argument that tips the scale of doubt into the range of absolute certainty. The odds are beyond chance. Biblical prophecies prove the divine intellect behind the Old and New Testament and confirms the inspiration of the Bible.

Prophecies are tricky business. Accurate 100 percent predicting of the future is humanly impossible. To set the stage, imagine this prophecy found in a time capsule from 500 years ago, in 1600 A.D. A document was found that a group of five different people all independently and accurately predicted the following future events:

1) A great man would be born in 1917.
2) He would be born in Massachusetts in a town called Brookline.
3) He would be elected president of the greatest nation in the world and become the world's most powerful leader.

4) He would be killed by a bullet to his head fired by a gun.
5) He would be buried in a nobleman's grave at Arlington Cemetery.

The man described is John F. Kennedy and all those facts came true. If these five men's writings were known and then this occurred, the world would be on alert and reading whatever else they predicted. While no one did foretell of John Kennedy's life and death, if they had the world would have certainly noticed.

As crazy as this all sounds, this and much more did happen with Jesus Christ and prophecy. This imaginary scenario about Kennedy was only a few predictions. Imagine hundreds of predictions like this that would all come true. With Jesus Christ, there were over 300 prophecies found in the Old Testament, written hundreds of years before his birth, that all came true. Not 280 out of 300, not 299 out of 300, but all 300.

One of the most game changing truths God leaves for the skeptic and seeker are the amazing prophecies about Christ throughout the Old Testament writings. Beyond coincidence? No doubt. Divine? Certainly.

If we examine the predictions and facts relating to the coming of the Messiah and how they came true with Christ, it should go a long way to proving the divine Bible and Jesus Christ as God's Son.

Job, Moses, David, Isaiah, Jeremiah, Daniel, and other Bible authors spoke of a Messiah and specifically about the coming Son of God. There are over 300 mentions of the coming Messiah in the Old Testament. Many of these predictions were things no one on earth could control, such as place of birth, manner of death, lineage, and what others did to him while he was being tried and crucified. Remarkably, they all came true. Not 90 percent or 80 percent, which would have been statistically nearly impossible by itself, but 100 percent.

Here is a table of just twenty-four prophecies that are found in the Old Testament, written hundreds of years before Christ was born, about the coming Messiah that all came through in Jesus Christ:

Sample of a few of the 300 Prophecies about Jesus from the Old Testament			
	Prophecies About Jesus	Old testament Versue	New Testament Fulfillment
1	Daniel has a vision in 490 years away, A messiah will come (70 "7's")	Daniel 9:24	Matthew 1:22
2	Messiah would be born in Bethlehem.	Micah 5:2	Matthew 2:1
3	Messiah would be born of a virgin.	Isaiah 7:14	Matthew 1:22-23
4	A messenger would prepare the way for Messiah (John the Baptist)	Isaiah 40:3-5	Luke 3:3-6
5	Messiah would be rejected by his own people.	Psalm 69:8	John 1:11
6	Messiah would be called a Nazarene.	Isaiah 11:1	Matthew 2:23
7	Messiah would speak in parables.	Psalm 78:2-4	Matthew 13:10-15, 34-35
8	Messiah would be sent to heal the brokenhearted.	Isaiah 61:1-2	Luke 4:18-19
9	Jesus would come to Jerusalem on a Donkey	Zechariah 9:9	John 12:12-16
10	Messiah would be betrayed by a friend	Psalm 41:9	Luke 22:47-48
11	Messiah's price money would be used to buy a potter's field.	Zechariah 11:12-13	Matthew 27:9-10
12	Messiah would be falsely accused.	Psalm 35:11	Mark 14:57-58
13	Messiah would be silent before his accusers.	Isaiah 53:7	Mark 15:4-5
14	Messiah would be spat upon and struck.	Isaiah 50:6	Matthew 26:67
15	Messiah would be hated without cause.	Psalm 35:19	John 15:24-25
16	Messiah would be crucified with criminals.	Isaiah 53:12	Matthew 27:38
17	Messiah would be given vinegar to drink.	Psalm 69:21	Matthew 27:34
18	Messiah's hands and feet would be pierced.	Psalm 22:16	John 20:25-27
19	Messiah would be mocked and ridiculed.	Psalm 22:7-8	Luke 23:35
20	Soldiers would gamble for Messiah's garments.	Psalm 22:18	Luke 23:34
21	Messiah's bones would not be broken.	Exodus 12:46	John 19:33-36
22	Soldiers would pierce Messiah's side.	Zechariah 12:10	John 19:34
23	Messiah would be buried with the rich.	Isaiah 53:9	Matthew 27:57-60
24	Messiah would resurrected from the dead.	Psalm 16:10	Matthew 28:2-7

What are the odds of this?

Could this all have been a series of lucky guesses and coincidences? It would be the most amazing coincidence in world history. Like the Big Bang Theory and life on this planet, it could have just happened, right? Is it mathematically possible as the Dream Team argues? If it is just hyperbole and coincidence, what about the prophecies? Is it possible? How would we handicap this when we look at the math?

The following probabilities are taken from Peter Stoner in "Science Speaks" (Moody Press, 1963) to show that coincidence is virtually ruled out by the science of probability. Stoner says that by using the modern science of probability in reference to eight prophecies, "We find that the chance that any man might have lived down to the present time and fulfilled all eight prophecies is 1 in 10 to 17th power. That would be 1 in 100,000,000,000,000,000." In order to help us comprehend this staggering probability, Stoner illustrates it by supposing, "We take silver dollars and lay them on the face of Texas. The silver dollars will cover all of the state two feet deep. Now mark one of these silver dollars and stir the whole mass thoroughly, all over the state. Blindfold a man and tell him that he can travel as far as he wishes, but he must pick up one silver dollar and find the marked one. What chance would he have of getting the right one? Just the same chance that the prophets would have had of writing these eight prophecies and having them all come true in any one man."

That is just eight prophecies of the over 300. Can you even begin to fathom the odds of 300 of 300 coming true with no single prophecy unfulfilled? It's amazing how God reveals himself to us through his word with the odds right in front of us.

Jesus Believed in the Bible

How else can we know the books of the Old Testament were the ones God wanted and should be trusted? Let's start with the fact that Jesus Christ believed in the Bible. He often quoted directly from the Old Testament Scriptures all throughout His ministry. He claimed the words in the Bible were more important than physical bread (Matthew 4:4). He believed that the Law and the Prophets were more sure than the heavens and earth (Matthew 5:17-18). He believed in the historical events of Lot with Sodom and Gomorrah (Luke 17:28-32), of Noah and the flood (Matthew. 24:37-38), of Jonah and the whale (Matthew 12:40-41), and of Daniel (Matthew 24:15). Jesus also believed that his chosen apostles would declare his word and teachings to the world after his departure and in doing so, recording the essence of the New Testament Scripture (John 14:26).

Closing Arguments on the Bible

The Dream Team tries to keep this argument simple. They repeat their original statement that we cannot rely on this book because the Bible is written by men filled with fiction and flaws and can be interpreted many different ways.

The Prosecution responds that the Bible is historically accurate and scientifically ahead of its time, accurate beyond belief. It is one of kind when it comes to history and science. It seems inspired in a way no other writing or story has ever been inspired. Could this all just be by chance? It might be if you believe in beating 750 trillion to one odds on history alone.

What about the prophecies of Christ and the coming Messiah? If 80 percent of the prophecies came true of the 300 or so, it would be considered amazing beyond comprehension. 100 percent would need to be true to pass the God test. 100 percent came true in Jesus Christ as the Messiah, proving the reliability and divine nature of the Bible, and making the odds of Jesus not being God's Son well beyond reasonable doubt.

The Prosecution submits that the odds, history, science, and amazing prophecy all defy the odds maker's ability to handicap this. The only logical explanation is this is God's Word and historical account of life on earth and our owner's manual to know God.

Dig in and Examine What the Facts Tell Us

Did the predictions and facts relating to the coming of the Messiah and how they came true with Christ prove the divine Bible and Jesus Christ as God's Son?
Could this all have been a series of lucky guesses and coincidences?
What are the odds of 300 of 300 coming true and then having no single prophecy unfulfilled?

It's amazing how God reveals himself to us through his Word with the odds right in front of us.

 Eric Metaxas is the New York Times #1 bestselling author of "Bonhoeffer," "Miracles," "Seven Women," "Seven Men," and "Amazing Grace." His books have been translated into more than twenty languages. He is the host of the Eric Metaxas Show, a nationally syndicated radio. Eric's *Wall Street Journal* op-ed, "Science Increasingly Makes the Case for God" is unofficially the most popular and shared piece in the history of the *Wall Street Journal*.[14]

---

[14] Web Site: ericmetaxas.com
Video and Audio Links: http://ericmetaxas.com/media/video/does-science-argue-or-against-god/

Chapter 7

The Empty Tomb: Conspiracy or Miracle?

The case is advancing nicely. There seems to be a good argument that in fact God created things. The Bible seems like a unique book that might be divine and might actually be God's words to us. The facts also point to Jesus actually existing and he seemed to be a wonderful man, but was he God? Was he God's Son or just a great prophet and teacher?

The death on the cross and his resurrection should help clarify this. What happened on the third day after he died? The Bible reports that after his unfair trial and crucifixion on the cross, the body of Jesus was wrapped in a linen cloth in accordance with Jewish burial custom. It was the custom that about 100 pounds of aromatic spices, mixed together to form a gummy substance, were applied to the wrappings of cloth about the body in that day and the body was placed in a solid rock tomb. In these times, it was customary with a tomb like the one Jesus was buried in that large stones weighing approximately two tons were normally rolled against a tomb entrance often using pulleys and levers to move the heavy stones.

Due to the worries of the Jewish leaders who condemned him, a Roman guard of strictly disciplined fighting men was stationed to guard the tomb so no shenanigans would take place. One of the guards affixed the Roman seal on the tomb which provided protection and a warning to anyone who might want to vandalize the tomb. If you broke the seal, you could incur the harsh wrath of the Roman Empire.

Despite all this, three days later the tomb was empty. The followers of Jesus reported he had risen from the dead. His followers claimed he appeared to them during a period of forty days after his death, showing himself to them by many "infallible proofs." The Apostle Paul recounted that Jesus appeared to more than 500 of his followers at one time, the majority of whom were still alive and who could confirm what Paul wrote.

The many security precautions that were taken with the trial, crucifixion, burial, entombment, sealing, and guarding of Christ's tomb makes it very difficult for critics to defend their position that Christ did not rise from the dead.

Even so, the Dream Team presents several theories into the empty tomb problem. First, the resurrection of Jesus could have been a hoax. The disciples could have stolen the body and this whole story of his resurrection and Jesus being God dies with them on the third day, with Christ. How can you know this empty tomb was not some major conspiracy by his followers to fool the Jews and lift up the Christians? We just can't know for sure and to base this entire case of him being God's Son on his rising from the dead is a weak link. The church created this resurrection to conveniently fit the narrative. Maybe it was just a tale that the early Christian's told, that grew over time to get people to believe the narrative.

The Empty Tomb: Conspiracy or Miracle?

"Regardless," the Dream Team asserts, "We cannot know for certain what happened, if he rose again or if his body was stolen. Given the lack of proof, the most logical explanation is not a miracle, but likely a conspiracy. So, to base everything on this one event with no proof, but the words of the disciples, cannot carry the day. Also, women discovered the empty tomb. Their witness and testimony must be discounted because they were not considered reliable witnesses, which was the custom of the day."

Why should we believe the resurrection?

The Prosecution stands to address this matter with a bit of a glow and anticipation. The Dream Team assert that the missing body never happened. The Jewish leaders of the day could have asserted this same thing, but they did not. Historical documents show that the grave was in fact empty and the Jewish leaders of the time acknowledged it and tried to discredit the reasons, further validating the empty tomb. That fact seems solid in history on both sides of the argument that we have an empty tomb both in the Bible and outside the Bible in historical documents. Let's put that point as a clear fact on the board as we progress. The tomb was in fact empty.

Now to the theories. Interestingly, the Jews and the Romans took extreme measures to seal the tomb and guard it with the Roman soldiers. The last thing they wanted was his body to be stolen and this movement to continue. They wanted this to all go away with his death and return to the way things were.

So, then what happened? Where was the body? The theory that the body was stolen by the disciples while the guards slept suggested by the Dream Team does not seem like behavior of scared, sad, and cowardly men. The sadness and fear of the disciples after Christ's death seems to make the theory of a brave and daring mission to face a team of soldiers at the tomb and steal the body highly unlikely. The disciples were in no mood to attempt anything like that. Even if they were in the mood, to pull it off would have been a big feat. Mission impossible on grand scale.

Another theory is that the Jewish or Roman authorities moved Christ's body. This is no more a reasonable explanation for the empty tomb than the theory of theft by the disciples. If the authorities had the body in their possession or knew where it was, when the disciples were preaching the resurrection in Jerusalem and Christianity was exploding, why didn't they stop the Jesus movement cold in its tracks? The Jewish leaders of the day certainly would have done everything in their power to prove a fraud given how far they went to kill Christ, yet no such thing happened? Why?

In the Book of Matthew, it reports that the soldiers came to the Roman and Jewish leaders and told them everything they saw. The truth would be too much to bear for the Jewish leaders who had just killed this man and who now may have arisen, so according to scriptures they paid the soldiers a large sum of money to spin a different tale. The story they told was they had fallen asleep and did not hear the tomb stone being rolled back. That was how the body was stolen. Actually, not very likely given the size and weight of the stone.

What Really Happened?

The defense presents Mark as the explanation of what happened. Here is how the book of Mark describes what happened at the grave in Mark 16:2-8

The Empty Tomb: Conspiracy or Miracle?

Very early on the first day of the week, they came to the tomb when the sun had risen. They were saying to one another, "Who will roll away the stone for us from the entrance of the tomb?" Looking up, they saw that the stone had been rolled away, although it was extremely large. Entering the tomb, they saw a young man sitting at the right, wearing a white robe; and they were amazed. And he said to them, "Do not be amazed; you are looking for Jesus the Nazarene, who has been crucified. He has risen; He is not here; behold, here is the place where they laid Him. "But go, tell His disciples and Peter, 'He is going ahead of you to Galilee; there you will see Him, just as He told you.'" They went out and fled from the tomb, for trembling and astonishment had gripped them; and they said nothing to anyone, for they were afraid.

First off, the fact that women were the first eyewitnesses of the resurrection is important. If the early church had made up the resurrection story, they would never have had their primary witnesses as women. At this time, a woman witness or testimony was not deemed credible. In fact, it was not even admissible in the court of law during this time. If they were going to fabricate a story, they would have picked a more trusted witness.

The Disciples – From Not Credible to On Fire, What Happened?

Secondly, the disciples went from Zeroes to Heroes overnight. These twelve men changed into the most supercharged advocates of Christ after this. Why? The changed lives of the disciples was a huge tell. If Jesus had not truly risen from the grave, the frightened, confused disciples would not have changed overnight and become fearless and impactful preachers. Nothing but a resurrected Jesus could have roused the original sceptics from their unbelief.

The Dream Team rises to raise a new point. They submit that perhaps certain parts of the Bible seem interesting and beyond dispute, but how could those in Jesus' inner circle turn their backs on God? This must prove that the witnesses are not only flawed, but not trustworthy to consider and they themselves were not sure of Jesus as God's Son. If they were not sure, why should we think we can have certainty? They were there with Christ and still doubted and did not see it clearly, so how can we be expected to today as we review this appeal?

The Dream Team might have found the flaw in the Christian story. How could these disciples not fight to the death for Christ after what they witnessed in miracles with Jesus? It seems unfathomable.

The Prosecution argues, the disciples' flawed human nature further proves the case of Christ. It seems unlikely the disciples would paint themselves as cowards and doubters since they were the authors. Might the story have been more convincing told like a modern day super hero tale of courage, strength, might, and willingness to die for the cause at all costs?

Peter, who was one of the Jesus' closely disciples, denied him three times when Jesus was facing wrath and trial. He was a big disappointment and the Bible reported his shortcomings. They were not concealed to make the story more believable. This is not a very convincing narrative to create a false faith through Peter and his fellow disciples. We would have expected to have more faith in Christ after all they had been through together.

Something big happened after the death and resurrection. The Christian faith movement picked up amazing momentum after Christ's

The Empty Tomb: Conspiracy or Miracle?

death and resurrection. What happened that changed everything? Why didn't this cottage faith die with Jesus on the cross?

After the death on the cross, the disciples sat in isolation until something happened that changed it all. Something happened that turned this men from regular people with fears, doubts, and questions, into the supercharged missionaries who told the story of Christ with such conviction that they were killed and stoned without ever retracting a word. What happened was not of this world!

Jesus Christ arose and appeared personally to the disciples. He also appeared to hundreds of others after his death. The tomb was empty and Jesus had returned. The disciples now understood. Their faith became complete, their flaws now bronzed over by the power of Christ's death and resurrection. The narrative was now clearly understood.

These disciples were turned into Superheroes with powers not known to them before the death on the cross. They were transformed. These men went from scared and weak to bold and filled with the Holy Spirit. Christianity rose on their wings as they boldly told the accounts of Christ, his life, his teachings, and his resurrection. It was their firsthand experience seeing the risen Christ with their own eyes that moved Christianity forward full speed.

Jesus went on to command them to preach the Gospel to all the world. They received wisdom and power from God through the Holy Spirit and the world changed. He was risen, he was risen indeed. Everything was true and Jesus was God living with us on earth. The disciples went on to share the news with extreme passion and power, and the Christian movement was started.

> **The transformation of the disciples, who went from cowards to martyrs and never again denying Christ after the resurrection, is bulletproof evidence of Jesus as God's Son.**

The truthful account of what they wrote in the Bible goes to show the disciples were not interested in looking good and fabricating the legacies, but in telling the story as it occurred, highlighting their flaws and faith gaps as they occurred. Jesus was truly God's Son on earth, willing to die for our sins. The Old Testament had promised it. It all came true and they now understood the entire narrative.

The Growth of Christianity

Being a Christ follower after Jesus died was very risky business with stiff penalties. No glamor and fame to walk this road. The Romans of the day did not accept this new movement and violently killed Christians. The disciples believed so much in the resurrection that they gave their lives to sharing the news. Prior to this, they ran and hid.

While they changed the world with their sharing of what happened, it did not end well for the disciples. The first disciple to die was James the brother of John, who was killed by the sword upon the order of King Herod (Acts 12:1–2). Church tradition holds that John miraculously survived being put into a cauldron of boiling water, then later was exiled to the Island of Patmos; Peter was crucified in Rome upside down; Matthew was slain by a sword in a distant city in Ethiopia; James, the son of Alphaeus, was thrown from a pinnacle of the temple, then beaten to death with a blacksmith's tool; Philip was hanged against a pillar at Hierapolis in Phrygia; Bartholomew was skinned alive; Andrew was bound to a cross—and preached to his persecutors until he died; Thomas was run through with a lance in the East Indies; Jude was shot to death with arrows; Matthias was first stoned and then beheaded; Mark died in Alexandria in Egypt after being cruelly dragged through the city. Through all the accounts, not one of the disciples changed their story or recanted their testimony when faced with violent death and consequences.

So, did Christ die, rise from the dead, and fulfill all of the Old Testament prophecies? Or was this all a legend that never happened? Was it a big cover up by the disciples to create a new religion? The most logical and reasonable explanation is that Jesus was God's Son, he came, he died, he arose on the third day, and appeared to the disciples and many others after his resurrection. It was the resurrection that changed them from flawed men to martyrs and superheroes of the Christian faith.

Yes, he arose indeed. Today, over 2 billion people identify themselves as Christian representing almost 1/3 of everyone living. Surely, something special happened 2000 years ago that leaves us where we are today.

Love was born and lived amongst us and this changed everything. It all came true, the prophecies were fulfilled. The odds are simply beyond chance.

Dig in and Examine What the Facts Tell Us

Something big happened after the death of Jesus on the cross. The Christian faith movement picked up amazing momentum.

What happened that changed everything?
Why didn't this cottage faith die with Jesus on the cross?
Was this all a legend that never happened?
Was it a big cover up by the disciples to create a new religion?
Or did Christ die, rise from the dead, and fulfill all of the Old Testament prophecies?

  I ask myself every day, "Am I Good Enough?" Christians claim that Jesus is the only way to heaven. But how could a good God, who created the entire universe in all its diversity, be so limiting? Is Christianity unfair? Isn't it more fitting to believe that good people from any religious or nonreligious background go to heaven, rather than people from one particular belief system? Maybe not, says Andy Stanley, founder of North Point Ministries. Find out why Jesus taught that goodness is not even a requirement to enter heaven and why Christianity is beyond fair.

Lots of people think Christianity is all about doing what Jesus says. But what if doing what Jesus says isn't what Jesus says to do at all? Jesus' invitation is an invitation to relationship, and it begins with a simple request: follow me.

Religion says "Change and you can join us." Jesus says, "Join us and you will change." There's a huge difference. Jesus doesn't expect people to be perfect. He just wants them to follow him. Being a sinner doesn't disqualify anyone. Being an unbeliever doesn't disqualify anyone. In fact, following almost always begins with a sinner and unbeliever taking one small step.[15]

---

[15] http://yourmove.is/episode/ep1-brand-recognition-2/

Chapter 8

Closing Arguments, Deliberations, and the Verdict

The main portion of the trial has been concluded. Now, the next step is the grand finale, the closing arguments. Lots of facts and testimony has been presented and the Justices are instructed to take this next step very seriously, as someone's life is in the balance. They are to step back, weigh the full body of evidence, deliberate, and come up with a binding verdict. As a Justice, you have to decide one way or another, you cannot abstain from voting on this.

Dream Team Closing

The Dream Team goes first. The arguments on the surface seem compelling. Science, says we must discount this God theory as we cannot prove it. More likely, we are the result of a random big bang of evolution and here we are. That is more believable then a divine creator. The facts say we cannot know if there is a god, thus we must refute. As they say, "If the glove does not fit, we must acquit." We are an enlightened society, science answers all of our questions and that is where we should put our trust.

The Bible is a great book for sure and a bestseller like no other, but it was not written by God, but by man and about man. It is a great compilation of fiction mixed with some historical facts, with many flaws, contradictions, and is not relevant for us today anyway. Jonah and the whale, Noah's ark, David and Goliath are stories we choose to put in the fiction category with some of the great works of Mark Twain, Hemingway, JK Rowling, and Michael Creighton. Can we take good parts from this book and live a better life? For sure, but can we look to the Bible as the word of God? No, we can't make that leap.

Jesus Christ, well that is an interesting story. Yes, he seemed to exist, to that we cannot refute, but God's Son? Maybe he was a great prophet, like Buddha, Mohammed or a great teacher like Gandhi or caretaker like Mother Theresa. Was he the one and only Son of God living amongst us? That story we cannot believe.

Yes, we've heard of prophecy. To us, this seems farfetched and our interpretation is different. Yes, the Bible talked of a Messiah, but Jesus was not the answer. We cannot prove that. It is just not certain.

Was Jesus falsely convicted? The Dream Team argues, "No. He claimed to be God's Son. That was blasphemy, so the punishment fit the crime and we cannot show enough proof to change that verdict rendered two thousand years ago. The sentence was a just sentence based on the facts."

The Prosecution Closes

Famous author CS Lewis once said, "Christianity, if false is of no importance, and if true, of infinite importance. The only thing it can't be is moderately important." As a Justice in this case, I strongly urge you to consider this case in the CS Lewis framework.

Closing Arguments, Deliberations, and the Verdict

Let's start with the easy part—God or no God? Science or creation? The amazing way our world was created, the intelligent design apparent everywhere we look, and the sheer beauty of it all point to a creator. It takes a great leap of faith to believe our world and all that is in it is not from God. The odds point to creation by a God and not random chance by a big margin.

Evolution or creation? From colliding rocks came life without a god? The Big Bang created humans, animals, and our unique universe with no creator? That seems farfetched. Intelligent design by an amazingly brilliant God is much more likely.

So, agreeing that there is a very compelling argument that there is a God and Creator, how did he chose to reveal himself to us? Could the narrative of God's love for us as told in the Bible be true?

History seems to back up the accuracy of the Bible beyond any doubt through historical societies, kings, and empires, all preserved with the accuracy of a Harvard historian. The Dead Sea Scroll discoveries prove the translations thousands of years later was 99.9 percent the same, even when transcribed by hand from generation to generation. Then there are the prophecies. Could this all be a big coincidence? The odds do not allow that possibility. The chances of 300 predictions coming true in one person are beyond reason and odds. Mathematically, it is impossible.

So, assuming we now can argue, there is a God and he did reveal himself to us through his Bible, then can we make the leap that Jesus was the Son of God and the Messiah predicted hundreds of years before he was born? The 300 prophecies came true. He was born in Bethlehem and died on a cross, without a broken bone, and rose again, just as the Bible predicted.

His life was nothing short of amazing with the miracles, healings, and amazing teachings. Interestingly, Jesus brought new teachings of a new system where the rules were changed and where two great commandments were the most important. Love God with all your heart and love your neighbor as yourself. Salvation and eternal life are not because of what we do, but what he did for us.

This salvation message was so simple that a criminal on the cross with Jesus believed as he was dying and Jesus promised him to later see him in paradise. What contrast to the old teachings of the time, where rules and works seemed to lead to God? Who was this Jesus? He certainly taught new things that rounded out the God narrative in such a loving way. Jesus died so we would not have to. His perfection made our flaws okay. We did not have to earn our way into heaven, he paved the way, and all it takes is belief. John 3:16 says, "God so loved the world, he gave his only begotten son, so that whoever believes in him shall not perish but have eternal life."

Clearly, Jesus was no mere man, he was not just a prophet, and he was not just a great teacher. He was either God himself as he claimed or the biggest fraud in the history of the world. You can't kind of be God. There is no middle ground on this claim.

So, as you consider the case, which one is it? The evidence and the odds point to a conclusion that should be clear: Jesus was God's Son and he was punished and killed unjustly despite the odds.

Like the OJ Simpson case, the odds of Christ being God's Son are overwhelming. The timelines fit, the motives make sense, the witnesses testified, and facts support it. Yes, a great Dream Team can make you doubt anything, but what does your heart say? What do the odds say? What do the facts say?

Jesus is God's Son and he was falsely convicted 2000 years ago by a system that could not consider all the facts. Reverse that wrong today.

Your Deliberations and Final Verdict

The facts are in, the case is closed, and now the system must decide. Deliberating is important. Consider the facts, consider the options, and think about the odds. You are the swing vote on this matter and your vote counts. Unfortunately, you can't leave the court room without reaching a verdict. Remember the words of C.S. Lewis, "This issue is of no importance if Jesus is not God's Son, but if it is true, it is of infinite importance. The only thing it can't be is moderately important."

Was OJ guilty? Most everyone today thinks so, but a few still doubt it. What do the facts say? Does the timeline and motive fit? Do we have good proof and credible witnesses? For OJ, the odds of him not being the murderer are off the charts. It is statistically impossible that there was another explanation, yet he walked out of that courtroom, in one of the most oddly unjust verdicts of recent time.

In the trial of Jesus Christ, which side of the verdict do you select? Was he guilty of blasphemy by falsely claiming to be God? If he was guilty of this, he was arguably the biggest fraud in the history of the world, leading more people astray than any other person who ever lived. What does the evidence say to you about this? How do you feel about it? The Dream Team in this world surely offer many issues that can cause doubt about God. It does require some faith and some belief, but proof exists to help that faith.

So, going back to the beginning, let's ask, does God even exist? The facts and science seem to strongly support this. Are humans living in a perfect Earth with all of the complexities of the universe as a random rock crashing, godless event or the result of a creator? Consider again the timeline and motive in this narrative. As you look at God as he has revealed himself, does this resonate? Could Jesus have coincidently fulfilled the prophecies and changed the world after his death and resurrection? Does another explanation make more sense to you? The prophecies in the Bible make the odds of Jesus being the Messiah and the accuracy of the Bible beyond mathematical chance. Combine the odds of our random earth being perfect as discussed with the multiple prophecies of Christ coming true 500 years later and you get odds of 1 in a trillion. Oddly convincing when you look at the facts.

Yes, pundits claim it could be random Big Bang, then evolution, then us, with no God, but mathematically that is oddly improbably. So if there is a God, who is he and what purpose would he have for us and why do we exist? Is his name Allah, Buddha, is he unknown and unrevealed to us or is he the God of the Nation of Israel, who created the earth, parted the Red Sea, saved Daniel from the lion's den, gave us Jesus Christ, and wants to spend eternity with us? Is he a God who showed the most amazing love by allowing his own Son to die a murderer's death, so we could be saved from our sins and flaws?

The amazing life of Christ is another area to ponder. The way he lived, the things he taught and lived out, and how he loved is truly seeing God in a way that anyone would be attracted to the love and compassion of God.

So, as you sit and thoughtfully now deliberate what is clearly the most important decision you will ever make in your life, the fact is, you must reach a verdict. The vote is either:

1) *Guilty, he was not God's Son, so he was lying, or*
2) *Not Guilty, he was punished for telling the truth and he is God's Son.*

Apathy and failure to seek the answer is the worst choice anyone can make in the quest to really know God. God promises that if you seek him, he will reveal himself to you. Faith can come in small steps like it did with the disciples. They were fishing one day and Jesus told them to drop their nets and join him. They did not fully understand God, Jesus, and the entire salvation story, but something led them to take the first bold step of exploration. God revealed himself to them over time, just like he will with you if you ask him. Truly seek him, the truth, wisdom, and peace in your beliefs about God and his Son, Jesus Christ.

Yes, there are always arguments on both sides and the Dream Teams of this world will always have their voice, but the pursuit of the facts and the consideration of both sides can lead you to a sound decision. Blind faith is not needed, the story of Christ and God's love will withstand scrutiny, deep review, and questions.

For many, faith is not a fact based exploration but a feeling. For those, consider yourself lucky if you have found God through Jesus Christ. For others like me, the journey to faith in Christ took questioning, exploration, and logic. It took looking at both sides of every argument and then considering the entire story. Does it make sense, what does the evidence point to, what are the flaws in the story?

A great place to start is in the life of Christ. The well known pastor from Atlanta, Andy Stanley Jr., has taught a solid theme around seeking to learn about the life of Jesus. Andy points out astutely that in the accounts of Jesus' life, even his early followers started with just a simple first step before truly believing. The disciples and many of the early followers of Christ did not really believe he was God's Son or get he was God himself. They were drawn to him by his teachings, his miracles, and his love. They were attracted to him by his qualities as God on Earth.

Their belief in him as the Son of God and pathway to God and eternal life was filled with doubts, stumbles, questions, and interesting chapters. When Jesus was taken away to his kangaroo court trial before he was crucified, the disciples were not world beaters standing up for him, but liars and cowards at that time, like most of us would be in that day. They were just flawed men, trying to figure it all out. After Jesus rose from the dead, it took him reappearing to the disciples for them to get the whole story. Thomas had to see his hands with the nail piercings to believe. Then they were truly Christ followers to their death. Andy argues wisely in his messages that the first step is to look at what Jesus taught and did.

Start with Jesus. What did he actually teach? How did he live his life? See if that resonates with you as a role model you can follow. Explore further and get your questions answered, dig in, study, learn, and leave no rock unturned. Blind faith is like a house built on sand. You may feel moved or touched by something you hear, read or see, but don't neglect the next steps of understanding what you believe, the objections to it, and then forming a firm foundation in your faith.

Read the book of John in the Bible and see what Jesus' life and teaching were all about. If you are a believer with some doubts or you are not living your faith, this is a great place to start to refresh what God taught us through his Son. If you are a seeker or unbeliever in Jesus, see what he is all about. The scriptures are amazing and stand on their own.

Maybe you know enough at this time to stand up and say, yes, I get it, I believe in Jesus Christ and the amazing God who created everything. The good news is simple. John 3:16 says, "For God so loved the world, he gave his only son, that whoever believes in him will not perish, but have everlasting life." Ask God into your life and everything you know will change.

It's important to know, God teaches he is not grading on the curve nor is he going to put your good deeds on a scale against your bad deeds and decide if you lived a good life and deserve eternal life. That's great news for us all. The death of Christ wipes away all of our wrongdoings and presents us to God as perfect, blameless, forgiven, and accepted.

Pastor Tim Lucas from Liquid Church in New Jersey preached a powerful lesson on how God sees us. He drew the analogy of a bride on her wedding day. When I saw the love of my life, Laura, walking down the aisle on our wedding day in that glistening white dress, she was beautiful, flawless, and my eyes could only see perfection. Tim Lucas drew the analogy to how God see's us in the same way after we accept Christ and our sins and flaws are forgiven. What an amazing analogy and what hope and joy comes for those who know Christ.

In Romans 3:23, the Bible teaches us the wages of sin are death, but the gift of God is eternal life through Jesus Christ our Lord. It is through faith, not works. We can't earn our way in, but we have to make a decision and that decision will change things forever, in this life and beyond. The road is narrow but the rewards are great. To be viewed by God as perfect and blameless, our sins long forgotten is an amazing picture of what the Bible teaches.

Faith – A Final Thought

Why is it that some people have faith and others, presented with the same information, have no inclination towards faith or a belief in God? Is it enlightenment? A desire to believe in something bigger than ourselves? Fear?

What is faith? The Bible defines faith in the book of Hebrews 11:1, "Faith is the assurance of things hoped for, the conviction of things not seen."

In Ephesians 2:8-9, Paul stresses that saving faith is a gift from God, "By grace you have been saved through faith; and that not of yourselves, it is the gift of God; not of works, so that no one may boast." These scriptures clearly show that faith comes from hearing and responding to the gospel. God uses people to present the gospel to others to accept or reject by free will faith.

Faith has been outlined to include three parts:
- **Intellectual.** Basic knowledge and understanding is required to have faith. True faith requires knowledge of things that are true and often wrestling over what is believed.
- **Conviction.** This is the inner emotional part of faith. Saving faith requires an inner conviction that the intellectual knowledge is true. Without conviction, faith falls flat.
- **Action.** This is the outward sign and proof someone has a saving faith. In James 2:20 it says, "Faith without works is dead." A person who hears the gospel and believes it to be true is still not saved unless he applies the gospel to himself. The lack of action proves one's faith is incomplete. True faith brings change.

So, how do you get faith? If you are struggling with religion, faith, and God, then try asking for faith as the first step. In Matthew 7:7, Jesus shared how you get faith. "Ask, and it will be given to you; seek and you will find; knock, and the door will be opened to you. For anyone who asks, receives; The one who seeks, finds; and the one how knocks, the door will be opened."

Often faith has a first step without fully understanding it all or believing it all. The disciples left their fishing nets behind and followed Jesus because of a beginning level of faith that he was something special. This faith grew over time as they learned more about Jesus, but their faith was not fully convicted until Jesus rose from the dead and reappeared. Their faith grew over time and was not instant. It had ups and downs, where they questioned Jesus, denied Jesus, and finally came to understand the entire picture.

Andy Stanley captures the essence in his book "Follow" in his sub title: *No matter what you believe, no matter how you behave, Jesus invites you to follow.* Faith is relational and powerful. Faith in Christ brings an inner peace and joy that can be found in no other place.

Dig in and Examine What the Facts Tell Us

Faith requires asking. Ask God to provide the capacity for faith.
Faith requires seeking, looking into the questions and answers, and forming a solid foundation for your faith. Faith requires knocking which is an action to find the answers by asking God. God promises if you ask for clarity, you will get it!
Lastly, God is love. He created us in his image and he wants a relationship with us. God wants the best for us and loves us unconditionally. Take a step towards God, through his Son, Jesus Christ today.

Cop buys birthday cake ingredients for shoplifting mother
By Crimesider Staff CBS News December 7, 2015

PORTSMOUTH, N.H. — A routine shoplifting investigation in southern New Hampshire gave way to an act of kindness when a police officer learned what a woman had stolen...and why.

According to CBS Boston, employees at the Ocean State Job Lot, a large discount store in Portsmouth, saw a woman shoplifting on November 19, and called police. Officer Michael Kotsonis was able to track the woman down from surveillance, the station says. He found out the woman had taken little more than some Crisco oil and vanilla frosting — what she said were ingredients for a cake for her daughter's birthday. Officer Kotsonis then returned to the store and purchased all of the ingredients and gave them to the woman. Assistant Store Manager Dan Rose said it wasn't something he expected from anybody.

"For somebody to pay for someone else's stuff is just amazing," Rose told CBS Boston. "It's above and beyond."

Fellow officers said it's typical behavior for the 19-year veteran of the force.

"[It was] pretty typical of this particular officer and a lot of police officers," said Lt. Darrin Sargent. "They don't look for recognition for the good things that happen. I think it happens more often than we know."

Officer Kotsonis spoke to the woman about the theft, making it clear he didn't condone it, CBS Boston reported.[16]

---

[16] © 2015 CBS Interactive Inc. All Rights Reserved.

Conclusion

Are You Still Deliberating?

Some of you still have more questions you would like to get answered. You want everything checked off before you consider something like this in your life. Here are a few thoughts to consider as you think about your faith and deliberate further.

A recent story has a very interesting parallel to God's love for us. In November of 2015, in Portsmouth, New Hampshire, a routine shoplifting investigation gave way to an act of kindness when a police officer learned what a woman had stolen and why. According to CBS Boston, employees at the Ocean State Job Lot, a large discount store in Portsmouth, saw a woman shoplifting and called police. Officer Michael Kotsonis was able to track the woman down from surveillance videos. He found out the woman had taken little more than some Crisco oil and vanilla frosting which she said were ingredients for a cake for her daughter's birthday, which she could not afford to buy. A sad tale of poverty and love for a child. Instead of arresting her and putting her in jail, Officer Kotsonis decided to return to the store, purchased all of the ingredients, and gave them to the woman.

If you think about it, this is what Jesus did for us, he paid a price for a sin he did not commit, on our behalf.

God's Motive

God created the heavens and the earth. It was not random rocks colliding. Man was imperfect and sinned and did not follow God's way. A holy God could not be in the presence of sin, so he lovingly sent his only Son, Jesus to make it right, to suffer for us, and make it so we could be in his presence eternally. A powerful gift that requires simple faith and acceptance. God wanted us to have free will to choose him and worship him.

God seeks a relationship where we not only love and worship him, but give back and love our neighbor and show God's love to others. Like the police officer in New Hampshire, Jesus paid the price for our wrongs, and showed love to us even when we did not earn or deserve it.

1) God created the heavens and earth.
2) Man was flawed and sinful so God could not be in the presence of sin.
3) Temple System with laws and rituals was the way to be close to God.
4) Messiah was predicted 700 years before he arrived with over 300 prophecies.
5) The predictions came true, Jesus was born, lived, died, and rose again.
6) His sacrifice for our sins paved the way to God with this one sacrifice for us.

7) The 600+ laws and commandments were replaced with grace and two important commandments Jesus emphasized: Love God with all your heart, and love your neighbor as yourself

8) Salvation and Eternal life with God come from faith and grace from God, not through our works or actions. We can't earn our way. We are not good enough and God does not grade on the curve. We all fail the test and salvation comes from pure grace.

9) There is only one road to eternal life, through Jesus Christ, God's Son as Jesus taught. It simply requires belief and faith. It's a free gift.

10) God provides eternal life and a life on Earth with inner peace and joy that cannot be compared. Salvation changes everything about how we want to live today.

Is God eternal? Was he always here? Who created him? How can he be everywhere at once, know our thoughts, etc.?

If God is who we think, then we cannot even grasp the way he thinks. I once heard an apt analogy. A cat was standing outside a garage door and sees someone push a button on a garage door opener, the door opens, and the cat enters the garage. How can the cat grasp all that went into the infrared beam, the motors, and more? The cat cannot grasp it and only knows the door opened. Think of God in the same way. We can only grasp a small part of what he is and why he does things. He has given us a certain capacity to understand and grasp things, but his truth and capacity is much different. Many things about God may not make sense now, but one day they will.

Trying to get it now is like the cat and the garage door opener. With many issues, our human understanding will come up short and we won't have the answers. That is okay. He has revealed what he wants and what we need at this time, but much of it is beyond our understanding. Things like disasters, kids dying at young ages, the pain of terrorism, brutal crime, what happened to that person in the hills of Viet Nam who never read a Bible must be left up to God. We must trust him and his justice and love, and realize we can only understand a small part of God and his thinking. One day we will have the answers when he reveals them. The one thing we can grasp hold of is his amazing love for us.

Don't all roads lead to God? This seems very judgmental.

All roads certainly lead to God, but not all of them lead to eternal life and acceptance by God. The Bible teaches you can't earn your way to God or be a good enough person to have God say, "Yes, you were the best." Jesus related, "I am the way, the truth and life, no man comes to the father, except through me." If we believe in God and in his Son, Jesus Christ, then the answer is clear, one road leads to eternal life. The road is narrow, but it allows all sinners who simply believe and accept him and his plan. Ultimately, only God will judge, but he tells us the rulebook clearly in His word and through His Son.

I am a good person, so at the end, I believe a loving God will weigh my good deeds compared to others and I am in.

Being a good person is admirable and a hope God has for all of us, but it does not overcome the sin issue. God teaches no one is good enough without Christ. Romans 6:23 teaches, that the wages of sin is death, but the gift of God is eternal life in Christ Jesus our Lord. So, while we might want to believe this is how it might work, it is not taught as the road to God in his word or through his Son, Jesus Christ. It is just wishful thinking and not founded in what God teaches. Why take a chance on missing out?

What about other faiths? Why is Christianity the only way?

Can we believe that all religions are equally true, when their definitions of who God is, how one is saved, and how God has revealed Himself are so contradictory? All roads cannot lead to heaven. Here is a simple way to look at other faiths from a historical and evidentiary standpoint to add to your thinking about different faiths and religions.

Christianity seems to be the only faith that is historically defensible. The basic claims of the Bible have historic basis and proof, as they are based on public events that can be historically verified. In contrast, the central claims of other world religions cannot be historically tested. They just have to be believed with blind faith. The believer in the Islamic faith has to trust in a private encounter Muhammad had, and this encounter is unable to be tested historically. It was him and his encounter.

For faiths like Mormonism, we have no way to truly investigate the claims of Joseph Smith and Mormonism and when we do, there are many questions that emerge. One man, 2000 years later having all of the rules and teachings of Jesus Christ updated? Enlightened?

Buddhism and Hinduism are not historic faiths, meaning they don't have central claims of events in time that can be explored and verified and confirmed. You either adopt their philosophy or you don't. There is no objective way to test them. Run through every religion that you know of and you will find this to be the case. Either it does not give historic details to the central event, the event does not carry any worldview-changing significance, or there are no historic events which form the foundation of the faith. The exception to this is Judaism, which is at the core of Christianity up until Christ came as the Messiah, when the faiths split.

Other religions started with a private dream about God or an angelic encounter with God or a private idea. Then, that one person told everyone what they saw. Christianity started with a public ministry of Christ with lots of eyewitnesses and written accounts of his life. He lived publicly, was crucified publicly, and rose from the tomb publicly. The public told everyone what they saw. It was not one man's revelation; it was much different.

I read stories the Old Testament about rules, about slaves, and the treatment of crimes. I can't believe in a God that endorses that.

Context is important to everything. Some of the Old Testament books talk about life in 2000 BC, and how the Jewish people were to be. They were filled with rules to help them know what was okay and what was not. God did not endorse slavery, but provided clear rules to treating "employees" or "slaves" with kindness and allowing them to be free after seven years. Parts of the Old Testament are history books about the life and times of the culture and how the people of faith, the Jewish people were to exist and cope. Remember, he eliminated the need to follow the 600 rules with his coming and death, and replaced these old rules with two, love God and love your neighbor as yourself. This is simple and covers most every situation we would encounter.

I don't like Christians, they are so judgmental and often the worst hypocrites. It is there way or the highway.

Don't judge Christ by a bunch of flawed and annoying Christians. We are all flawed, imperfect, and often annoying. Our passion for our faith can lead to overbearing sharing, but it is because of the beliefs we have and the love we have for our family and friends to share the eternal journey. The nature of God and Christ is amazing. We are taught not to judge and we try not to. Only God judges and he has laid out the way it will work in his word. Discover for yourself what he tells you in his word.

What about new Religions and Hybrid and Spinoff Christian Faiths that have added new teachings from Prophets and Seers not found in Jesus teachings or in the Bible?

Jesus is God's Son and God himself. I don't think he needs any new editions or revisions to his teachings. Man's attempt to add rules, revelations, and teachings to the Bible are not from God. Man screws things up when we try to add rules, regulations, and new concepts that are not from Christ and from the Bible. You can keep faith pretty simple if you start with Jesus and his message and stay there. The Gospels of Mathew, Mark, Luke, and John will give you four accounts of his life and teachings. These are filled with all you need to know about God and his love for us.

Man's attempt to clarify or add to the Bible with our own ideas of how we should do things, or listening to "leaders" who change things through their own revelations that are not consistent or in the Bible need to be discounted and discarded. If you believe in God, his power, his Son, it's hard to believe he would need any help later clarifying things or changing rules to suit a new generation.

Faith is simple, it is Christ through grace with a few simple guidelines to live as Christ would want us to live. Jesus taught there is no "qualifying" or good deeds that get you in or mortal sins that prevent your entry. The robber murderer who was crucified beside Jesus, believed and was promised Jesus would see him in heaven that very day.

I believe in the God of my own understanding – I have a relationship with God.

Sounds like you are on your way to knowing God, but according to Jesus Christ, God has a name and he sent his Son and there is only one way to him. He does not teach there are many gods and many roads. The Bible teaches there is one God, with one Son, and one truth, so everything can't be right. However, it sounds like God is revealing himself to you so ask for wisdom. He will grant it to you to find him. Ask for faith and he will give it to you. Ask for clarity and it will arrive.

Matthew 7:7 says, "Seek and you will find, knock and the door will be opened you."

Revelation 3:23 says, "I stand at the door and knock, if anyone hears my voice and opens the door, I will come in and be with him."

So, what is your final verdict?

Appendix

Discover More Online: Oddlyunjust.com

Great Resources for More Inspiration

Here are a few of my favorite places that bring great content to better understand faith, God, and grapple with the tough questions in life about these topics. You can download content to listen to them as podcasts, books on tape, watch videos or download and read some great books on the topic of God from some gifted speakers, authors, and communicators. These are all highly recommended sources for knowledge and wisdom to help you in your faith journey.

Author Lee Strobel

Atheist-turned-Christian Lee Strobel, the former award-winning legal editor of *The Chicago Tribune*, is a *New York Times* best-selling author of more than twenty books and serves as Professor of Christian Thought at Houston Baptist University. Described in the *Washington Post* as "one of the evangelical community's most popular apologists," Lee shared the Christian Book of the Year award in 2005 for a curriculum he co-authored with Garry Poole about the movie *The Passion of the Christ*. He also won Gold Medallions for *The Case for Christ, The Case for Faith*, and *The Case for a Creator*, all of which have been made into documentaries distributed by Lionsgate.

- Web Site: www.leestrobel.com
- Books: A Case for Christ, A Case for Faith
- Video Link: the Case for Christ video link–https://vimeo.com/17960119

J. Warner Wallace

J. Warner Wallace was an atheist for thirty-five years. He was passionate in his opposition to Christianity, and he enjoyed debating his Christian friends. In debating his friends, J. Warner seldom found them prepared to defend what they believed. He became a Police Officer and eventually advanced to Detective. Along the way, he developed a healthy respect for the role of evidence in discerning truth, and his profession gave him ample opportunity to press into proactive what he had learned about the nature and power of evidence. Throughout all of this, he remained an "angry atheist," hostile to Christianity and largely dismissive of Christians. From angry atheist, to skeptic, to believer, to seminarian, to pastor, to author, and podcaster, his journey has been assisted by his experience as a Detective. J. Warner wrote, "Cold-Case Christianity" with a desire to share those experiences with you,

- Web Site: www.coldcasechristianity.com
- Book: *Cold Case Christianity*
- Video and Audio Links: the web site has great links to videos and audio on the great questions around Faith

Andy Stanley

Andy Stanley is an amazing Communicator, author, and pastor. He founded Atlanta-based North Point Ministries in 1995. Today, NPM is comprised of six churches in the Atlanta area and a network of thirty churches around the globe, collectively serving over 60,000 people weekly. A survey of U.S. pastors in Outreach Magazine identified Andy Stanley as one of the top 10 most influential living pastors in America.

- Web Site: Yourmove.is
- Books: Multiple Books
- Video and Audio Links: Many great series exist on the web site to watch and listen to on all topics around Faith. I suggest you start with the series, Christian. Here is the current link from this site on this series: http://yourmove.is/episode/ep1-brand-recognition-2/

Eric Metaxas

Eric Metaxas is the New York Times #1 bestselling author of "Bonhoeffer," "Miracles," "Seven Women," "Seven Men," and "Amazing Grace." His books have been translated into more than twenty languages. He is the host of the Eric Metaxas Show, a nationally syndicated radio. Eric's *Wall Street Journal* op-ed, "Science Increasingly Makes the Case for God" is unofficially the most popular and shared piece in the history of the *Wall Street Journal.*

- Web Site: ericmetaxas.com
- Book: "Miracles, Everything You Always Wanted to Know About God, But Were Afraid To Ask"

- Video and Audio Links: http://ericmetaxas.com/media/video/does-science-argue-or-against-god/

Tim Lucas

Tim Lucas is pastor, speaker, and founder of **Liquid Church**, one of the fastest-growing churches on the East Coast. Every Sunday, over 3,000 people hear Tim preach at one of Liquid's metro area campuses. A dynamic communicator, Tim is known for his trademark humor, honesty, and insight. A graduate of Wheaton College, Tim is known for his creative use of story, scripture, and multimedia to communicate life-changing truth. Liquid Church's innovative approaches to outreach have been spotlighted by *CNN* and *The New York Times*.
- Web Site: http://www.pastortimlucas.com/
- Video and Audio Links: 100+ teaching Podcasts exist that are easy to listen to about Faith. Free Audio Download Links: https://itunes.apple.com/us/podcast/liquid-church-pastor-tim-lucas/id82361706?mt=2

About the Author

Larry Hartmann is a successful entrepreneur and first time author. A graduate of the business school at Cal State Fullerton, Larry founded a specialty finance company with three partner's right out of college. The business was recognized as an INC 500 growth company and later was taken public on the Nasdaq and was ultimately sold to a Dow 30 Company. Larry currently is the CEO of ZRG Partners, a global executive search firm with offices throughout the world. Hartmann has also served on the board of directors for public and private equity backed business as well as academia. He is currently the chairman of the board of Impact Paterson, a faith-based, not-for-profit organization that focuses on creating jobs for the needy and marginalized in Paterson, New Jersey.

Larry resides in New Jersey with his wife and has three sons.

Contact: larryhartmannzrg@gmail.com

CPSIA information can be obtained at www.ICGtesting.com
Printed in the USA
BVOW06s1932220416

445293BV00003B/4/P